50 FINDS FROM MANCHESTER AND MERSEYSIDE
Objects from the Portable Antiquities Scheme

Vanessa Oakden

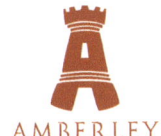

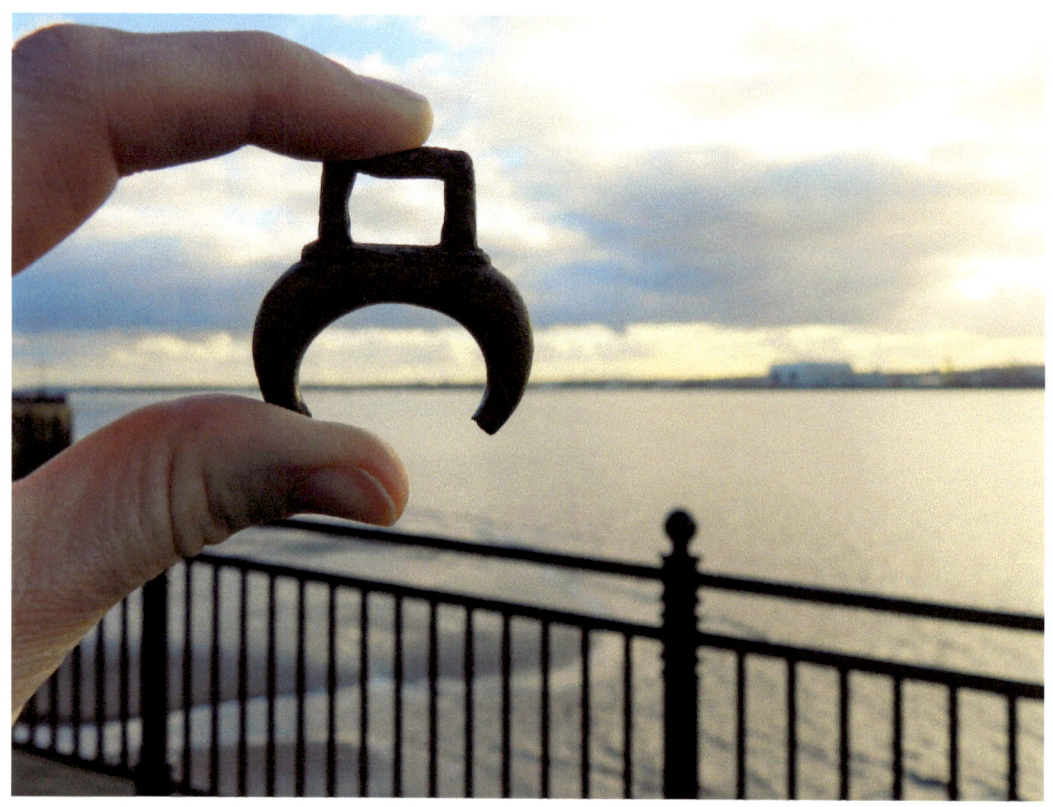

First published 2016

Amberley Publishing
The Hill, Stroud
Gloucestershire, GL5 4EP

www.amberley-books.com

Copyright © Vanessa Oakden, 2016

The right of Vanessa Oakden to be identified as the Author of this work has been asserted in accordance with the Copyrights, Designs and Patents Act 1988.

ISBN 978 1 4456 5855 1 (print)
ISBN 978 1 4456 5856 8 (ebook)

All rights reserved. No part of this book may be reprinted or reproduced or utilised in any form or by any electronic, mechanical or other means, now known or hereafter invented, including photocopying and recording, or in any information storage or retrieval system, without the permission in writing from the Publishers.

British Library Cataloguing in Publication Data.
A catalogue record for this book is available from the British Library.

Typeset in 10pt on 13pt Celeste.
Typesetting by Amberley Publishing.
Printed in the UK.

Appointed GPSR EU Representative: Easy Access System Europe Oü, 16879218
Address: Mustamäe tee 50, 10621, Tallinn, Estonia
Contact Details: gpsr.requests@easproject.com, +358 40 500 3575

Contents

	Acknowledgements	5
	Foreword	7
	Preface	8
	Introduction	10
Greater Manchester		12
1	Prehistory (500,000 BC–AD 42)	13
	Bronze Age (2350–801 BC)	16
	Iron Age (800 BC–AD 42)	22
2	Roman (AD 43–409)	29
3	Early Medieval (AD 410–1066)	39
4	Medieval (1066–1539)	45
5	Post-Medieval (1540–1900)	52
Merseyside		58
6	Prehistory (500,000 BC–AD 42)	59
	Neolithic (4000–2351 BC)	61
	Bronze Age (2350–801 BC)	63
7	Roman (AD 43–409)	66
8	Early Medieval (AD 410–1066)	74
9	Medieval (1066–1539)	77

10	Post-Medieval (1540–1900)	84
	Concluding Thoughts	94
	Further Reading	96

Acknowledgements

This book has been made possible due to the work of the Portable Antiquities Scheme (PAS) through which I have recorded archaeological objects since 2008. I would like to thank the PAS for supporting me in my work and in the writing of this book: Michael Lewis, Claire Costin, Ian Richardson, Sally Worrall, John Naylor, Helen Geake, Kevin Leahy, and Sam Moorhead and, of course, all my fellow FLOs past and present. Special thanks to Peter Reavill and Dot Boughton. I would like to thank the Museum of Liverpool for their support of PAS and my role as FLO; in particular, Janet Dugdale, Jen McCarthy, Liz Stewart, Jeff Speakman, Mark Adams, Clare Ahmad, Ron Cowell and Susie White. Thanks to my volunteers who make a huge difference to my work. I would like to thank the following who allowed me to access their finds or shared their images: Manchester Art Gallery, Bryan Sitch and Irit Narkiss at Manchester Museum, Ian Trumble at Bolton Library and Museum Services, Peter Ogilvie at Salford Museum and Art Gallery, Julia Farley and Eleanor Ghey at

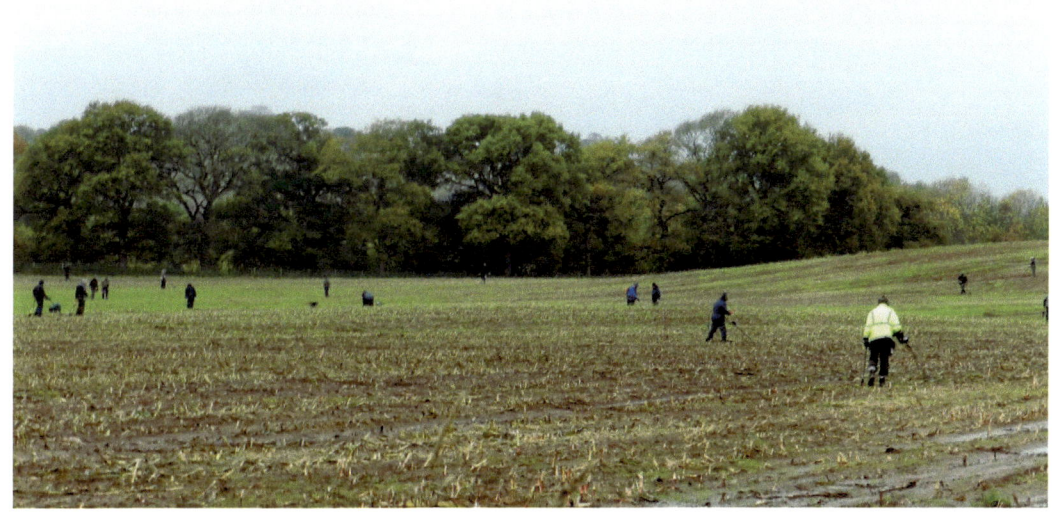

the British Museum, Murray Andrews, Anna Lewis, Ross Trench-Jellicoe, Andy Brown and Bob Johnston. Thanks to Daniel Pett, who built and maintained the current PAS database at the British Museum. Manchester Histories Festival has greatly added to my knowledge of Manchester's archaeology and thanks are due to Mike Nevell, Noman Redhead and Andy Myers at the University of Salford in the Centre for Applied Archaeology. Thanks to Birgitta Hoffman for identifying many beads and sharing her knowledge. Finally a huge thank you to all those who have recorded their finds with the Portable Antiquities Scheme, without whom this book would not have been possible.

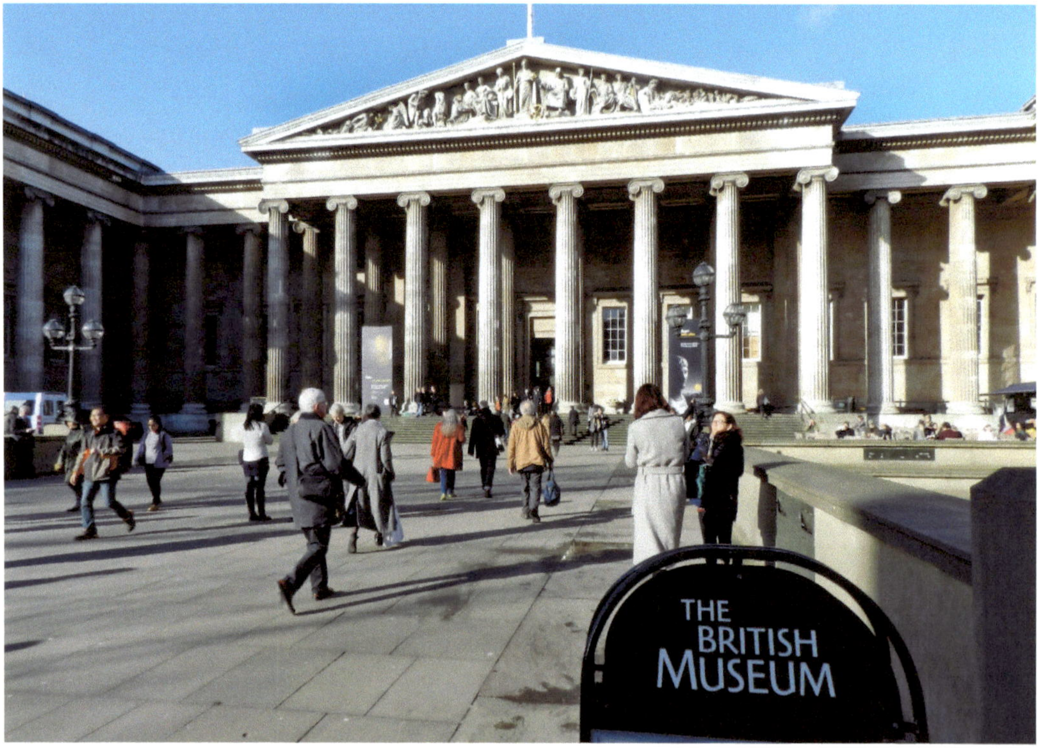

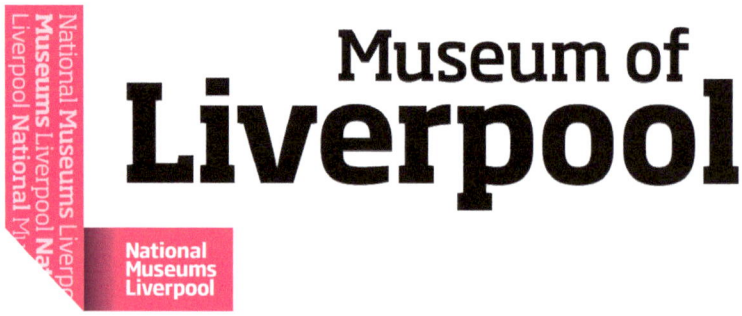

Foreword

The places in which we live and work have a long past, but one that is not always obvious in the landscape around us. This is a forgotten past. Most of us know little about the people who once lived in our communities 50 years ago, let alone 500, or even 5,000 years past. Like us, they lived, played and worked here, in this place, but we know almost nothing of them...

History books tell us about royalty, great lords and important churchmen, but most others are forgotten by time. The only evidence for many of these people is the objects that they left behind; sometimes buried on purpose, but more often lost by chance. Occasionally, through archaeological fieldwork, we can place these objects in a context that allows us to better understand the past, but nowadays excavation is mostly development led, and so only takes place when a new building, road or service pipe, is being constructed.

A unique way of understanding the past is through the finds recorded through the Portable Antiquities Scheme, of which those chosen here by Vanessa Oakden (Finds Liaison Officer for Cheshire, Greater Manchester and Merseyside) are just fifty of over 6,176 objects from Greater Manchester and Merseyside on its database (www.finds.org.uk). These finds are all discovered by the public, most by metal-detector users, searching in places archaeologists are unlikely to go or otherwise excavate. As such they provide important clues of underlying archaeology that (once recorded) help archaeologists understand our past – a past of the people, found by everyday people.

Some of these finds are truly magnificent, others less imposing. Yet, like pieces in a jigsaw puzzle they are often meaningless alone, but once placed together paint a picture. These finds therefore allow us to understand the story of people who once lived here, in Greater Manchester and Merseyside.

Dr Michael Lewis
Head of Portable Antiquities & Treasure
British Museum

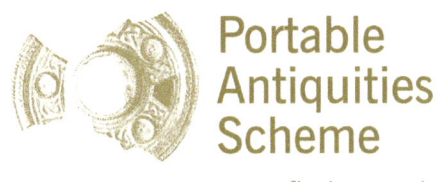

Preface

The Portable Antiquities Scheme (PAS) is a voluntary scheme set up to record archaeological objects found by members of the public in England and Wales. It is funded by the department of Culture, Media and Sport through the British Museum and has a network of Finds Liaison Officers whose role is to record these finds. Archaeological objects can tell us about the local economy, manufacturing skills and fashion, and they can help us identify areas of activity, where battles took place and the story of everyday life. By carefully plotting the find spots of these objects we can identify patterns that tell us about life in the past.

PAS recorded its millionth object in 2014 and the numbers are growing steadily. Since 1997 a Finds Liaison Officer has been working with National Museums Liverpool, recording chance finds. By 1 January 2016, 14,213 objects had been recorded by the scheme in Liverpool, providing a fantastic resource to be used by researchers and members of the public who want to learn more about the past. These are not just locally found objects, but also objects found in other counties by local people. This book has been divided into two parts, highlighting some fantastic and interesting finds from Greater Manchester and Merseyside, with finds arranged chronologically within each part. Further information on each find in this book can be found on the PAS database, www.finds.org.uk/database, by entering the unique finds reference number, e.g. LVPL-039CF2.

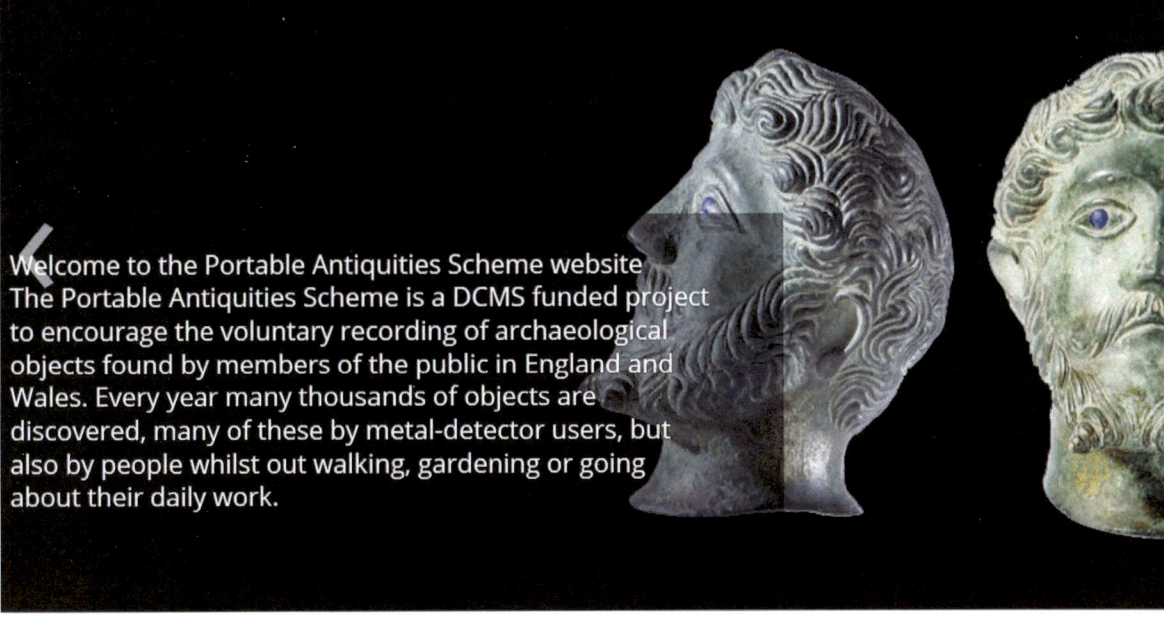

Welcome to the Portable Antiquities Scheme website
The Portable Antiquities Scheme is a DCMS funded project to encourage the voluntary recording of archaeological objects found by members of the public in England and Wales. Every year many thousands of objects are discovered, many of these by metal-detector users, but also by people whilst out walking, gardening or going about their daily work.

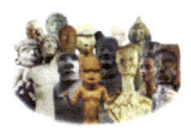 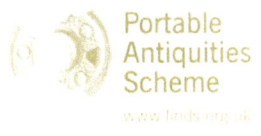 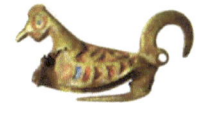

Portable Antiquities Scheme

Introduction

Greater Manchester and Merseyside are both relatively new counties. Today Greater Manchester is made up of several boroughs, which include Bolton, Bury, Manchester, Oldham, Rochdale, Salford, Stockport, Tameside, Trafford, and Wigan. Prior to the creation of Greater Manchester on 1 April 1974, the area was known as South East Lancashire and North East Cheshire, and included eight independent county boroughs and some of the West Riding of Yorkshire.

Like Greater Manchester, Merseyside is also a fairly modern construct, which today includes Knowsley, Liverpool, Sefton, St Helens and Wirral. Both counties came into being following the introduction of the Local Government Act 1972. Prior to this, the current area of Merseyside was made up of Lancashire, Cheshire and six self-governing county boroughs.

Although we naturally try to define our landscape with labels and boundaries, people are not restrained by them. Likewise, objects from the past did not remain within borders; instead they travelled across landscapes, brought by people spreading new ideas in design, technology and beliefs. As the Finds Liaison Officer for Greater Manchester and Merseyside, I have chosen fifty finds discovered within these borders, allowing us a glimpse of the stories these counties hold. Today Greater Manchester and Merseyside are hubs of activity, homes to trade, industry, and inspiring cultural centres. They are also largely built up through modern urbanisation. Great swathes of our past landscape lie beneath our modern roads and buildings, inaccessible to modern archaeologists until construction work opens a small window, allowing us a patchwork view. Yet in and around these cities and suburbs lie pockets of farm land, rural areas and plenty of gardens. It is here where objects from the past are often discovered, reminding us of what went before.

The aim of this book is to highlight fifty fantastic finds from Manchester and Merseyside. In doing so we celebrate our communities, both past and present, and those who chose to responsibly record their finds.

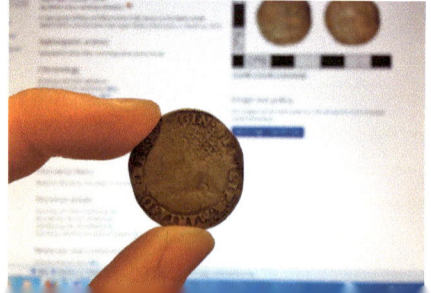

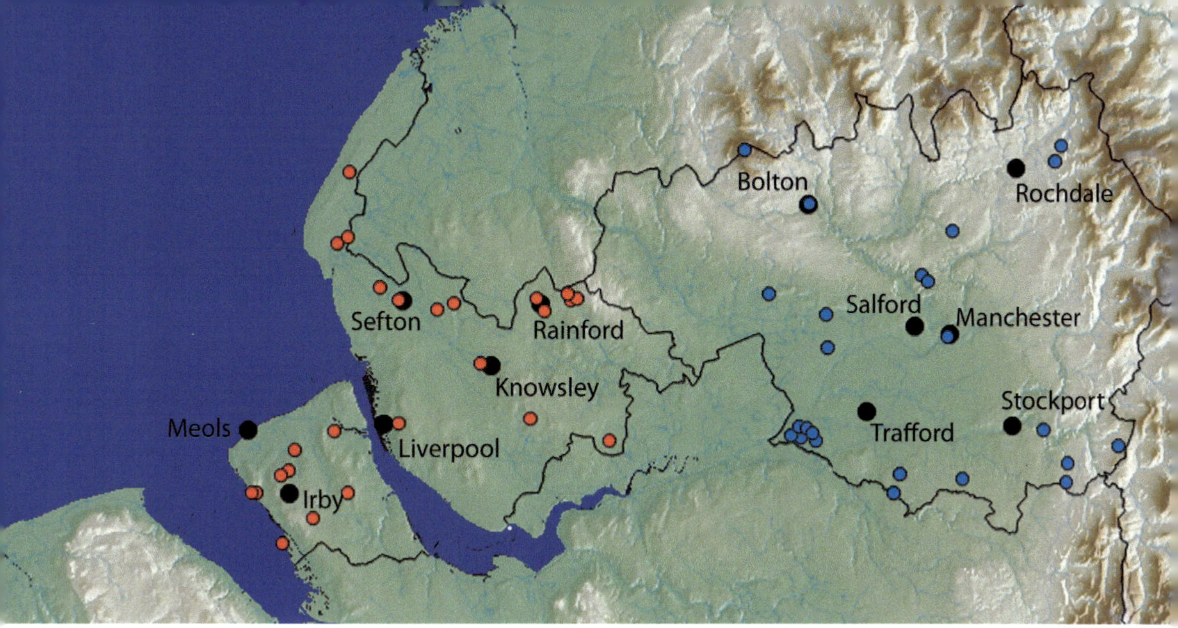

Map showing fifty finds from Manchester and Merseyside, kindly provided by Peter Reavill. (Contains OS data © Crown copyright [and PAS database right], 2016)

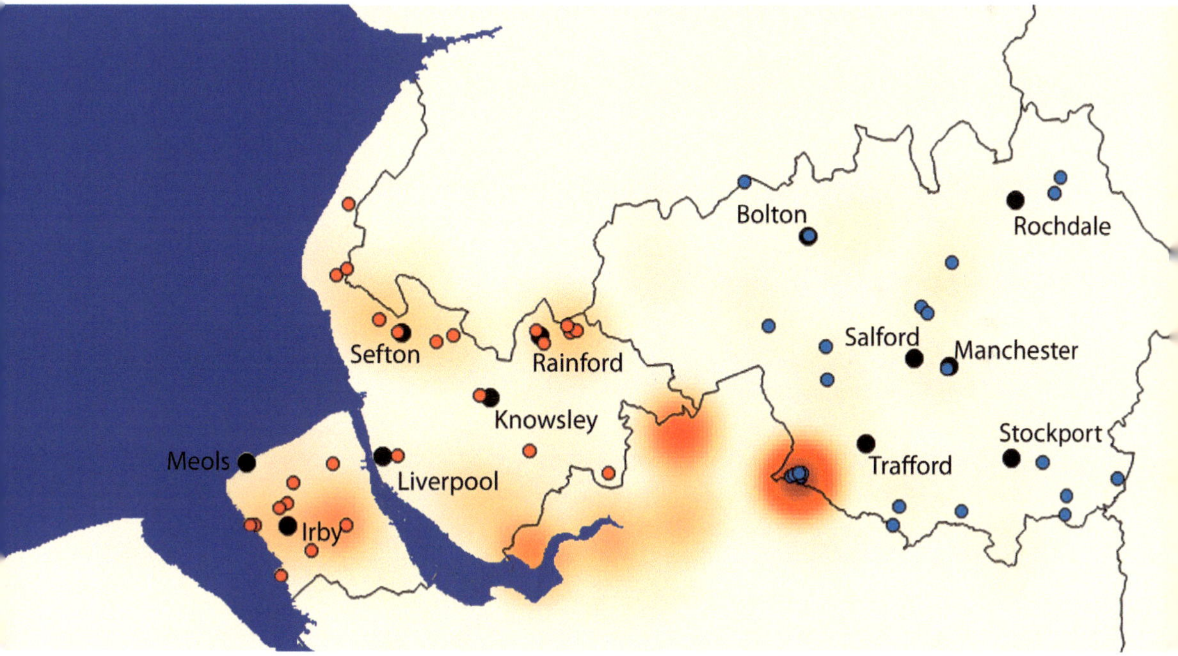

Heat map of the fifty finds, mapped against principal places and all finds reported to PAS. (Contains OS data © Crown copyright [and PAS database right], 2016)

Part 1
Greater Manchester

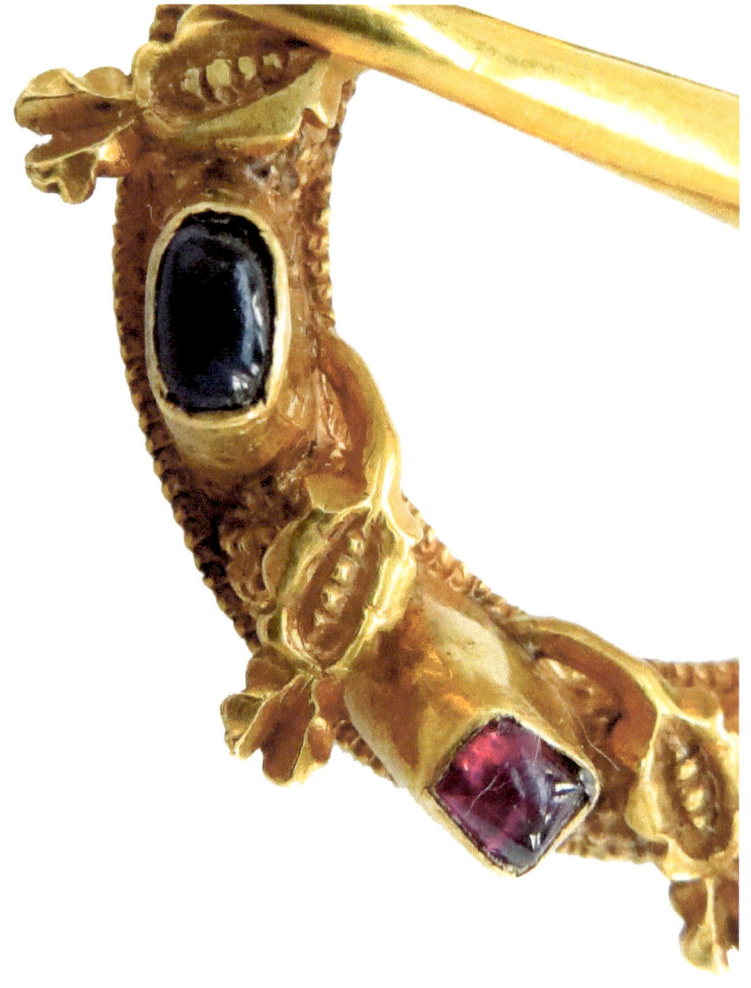

A detailed view of the gold and gem brooch discovered in Victoria Street in 1971.

Chapter 1
Prehistory (500,000 BC–AD 42)

In Greater Manchester our evidence for early prehistoric activity is mostly limited to scatters of flint and stone artefacts, including a Mesolithic group from Rochdale. Through the research of Dr Andrew Myers, University of Salford, these assemblages reveal part of the living pattern of people during this period. Mesolithic hunter-gatherers travelled between the lowlands of the Trent Valley, transporting cores of unworked flint to upland sites in the Pennines. Here they were knapped to make complete tools like harpoons and arrowheads. Once made, these tools were brought to the top of the Pennines, where they were used to hunt red deer. The resulting antler, hides, sinew and meat could, in turn, be transported back to the lowlands. The location of these flints has been vital in piecing together this evidence. Likewise, when recording chance finds, it is essential to record accurate findspots, in order that the data can be used.

The careful recording of flint scatters with accurate findspots and descriptions allow archaeologists to study and understand the activities of prehistoric people in much greater depth. Changes in technology and excavation techniques also allow sites to be re-examined and rediscovered. A great example of this is the Bronze Age site of Shaw Cairn, which is positioned on a projecting headland on Mellor Moor overlooking the Cheshire plain. Originally the site was excavated in the mid-1970s, leading to the discovery of a series of chambers and cremation cists. The cairn was recently re-excavated during successive seasons from 2008 to 2014. During the 2008 excavations a stone-lined cist was discovered; the bones had long since rotted away, but a distinctive stain in the form of a crouched burial was observed. Also found were a flint plano-convex knife and a rare amber necklace.

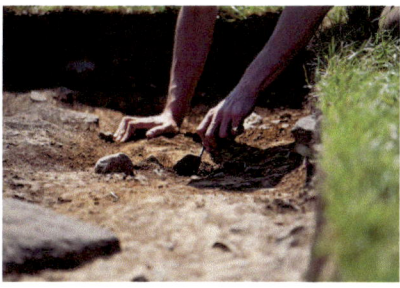

Excavations at Shaw Cairn, Mellor.
(Andy Brown)

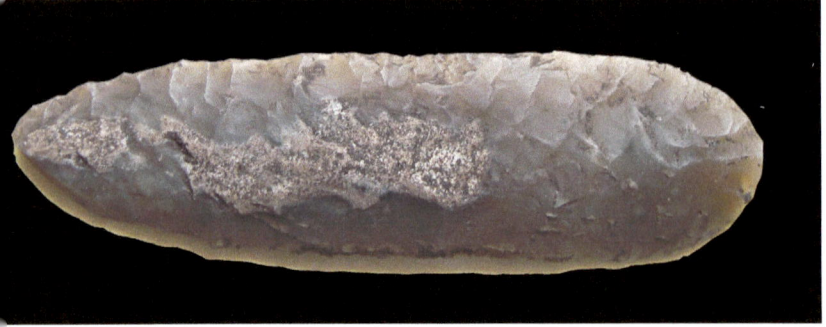

Left: Flint plano-convex knife. (Dr Andrew Myers)

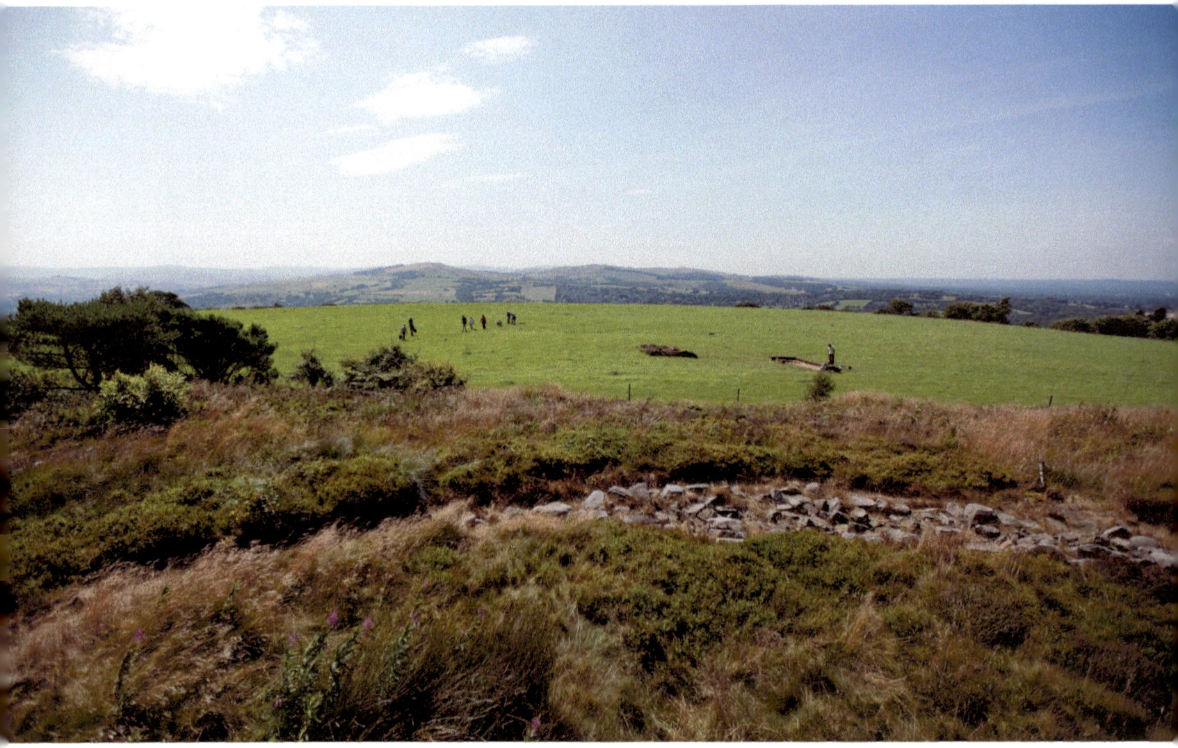

The view from Shaw Cairn looking southwards towards the hills of the western Peak District. (Andy Brown)

The position of Mellor in the landscape is significant. Using the river-valley routes, Mellor provides an important link between the Peak District and the lowlands.

These sites cannot be fully understood in isolation, but become clearer within their wider landscapes. As well as providing valuable archaeological data in their own right, chance finds such as the Bronze Age flaked dagger from Horwich provide important supporting evidence for how these early communities lived, worked and interacted.

Early stone axes and later metal ones were important tools with a practical function; however, they also speak of wealth and social status, and would have been treasured by those who owned them. The people who occupied the area around Shaw Cairn, as well as other local prehistoric sites, would have been using the tools seen below.

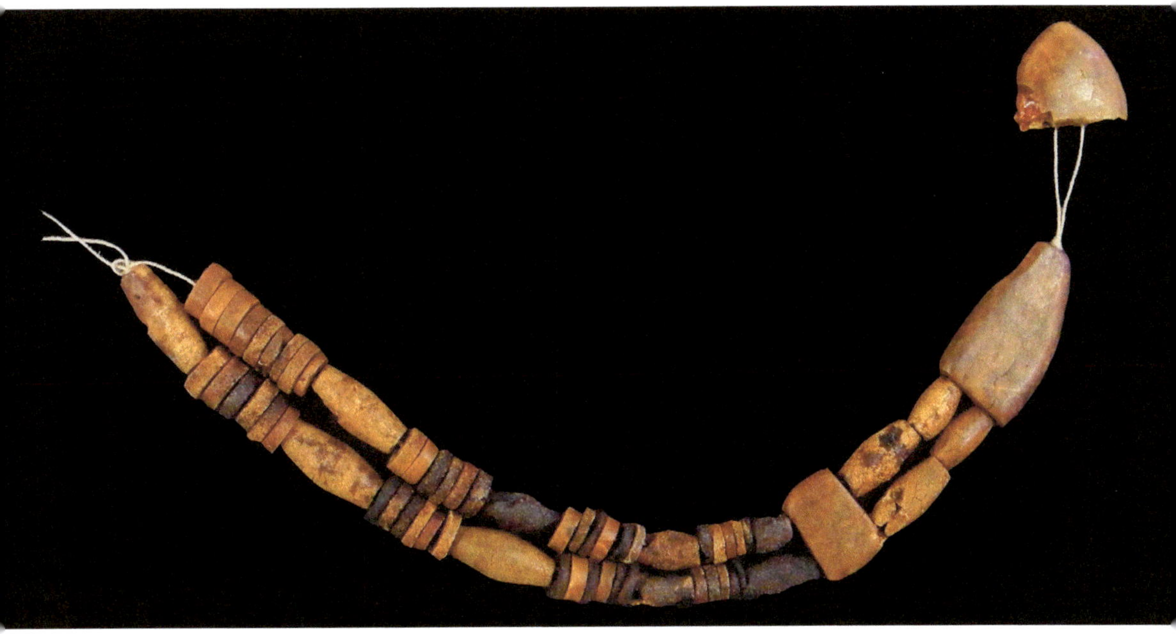

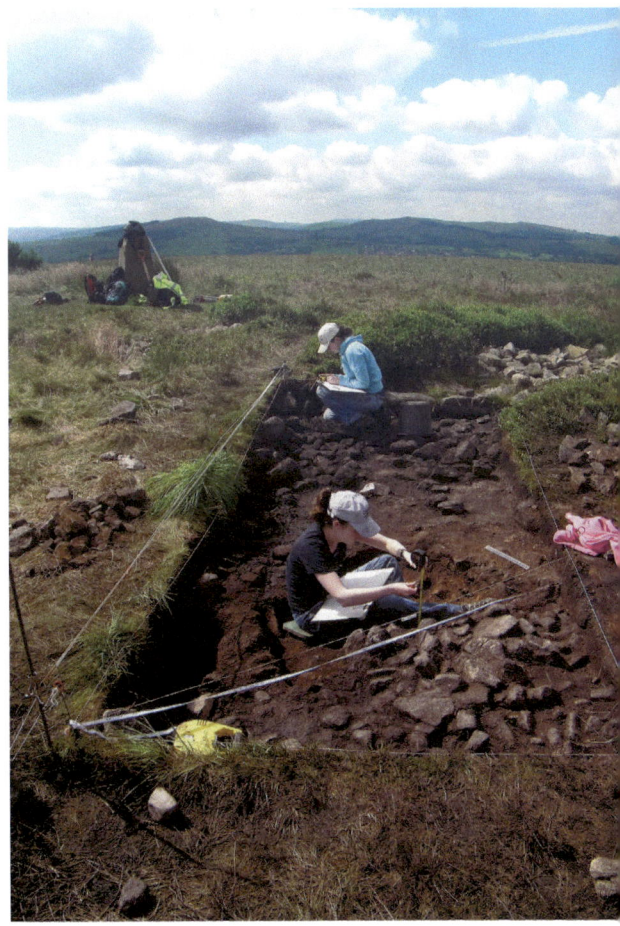

Above: The Shaw Cairn amber necklace, as reconstructed by Alison Sheridan. (Alison Sheridan)

Right: Vanessa Oakden (foreground) and Samantha Rowe (background) recording part of Shaw Cairn, during the 2012 excavation. (Dr Bob Johnston)

Bronze Age (2350–801 BC)

1. Flint dagger (LVPL-F7E419)
Early Bronze Age (2500–1500 BC)
Discovered in 1996 in Horwich. Length 141 mm.

This flaked dagger has been painstakingly crafted to create both a useful tool and beautiful object. The flint is flaked on each face with covering retouch. Along each long edge and around the point is short, parallel low-angle retouch. Flint daggers were introduced with what is known as the 'Beaker package'. This package, introduced by the Bronze Age Beaker people and named after their style of pottery, included the ability to work mysterious metals such as copper, bronze and gold, as well as religious beliefs and new artefacts such as daggers. This flint dagger may represent a copy of one of the earliest metal daggers and is one of the rarest types of Bronze Age flint implements found in Britain.

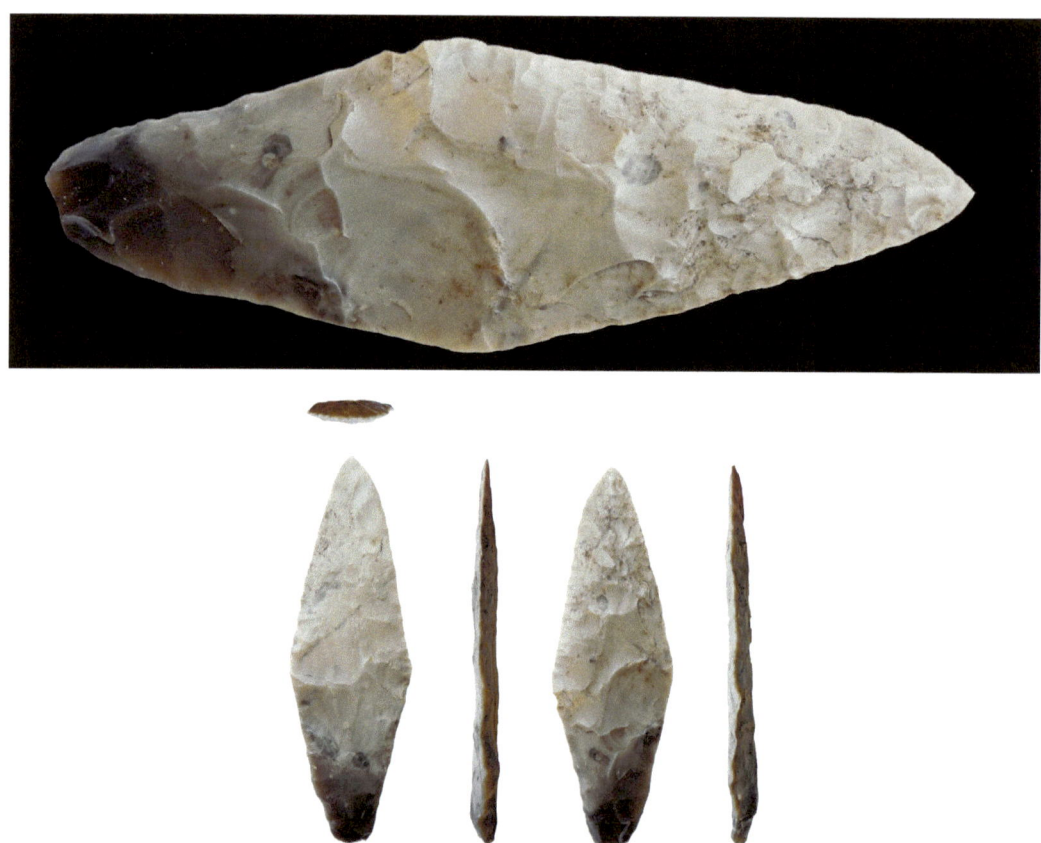

2. Copper-alloy flat axe head (LVPL-A626B1)
Early Bronze Age (2300–2050 BC)
Discovered in 2013 in Altrincham. Length 80.03 mm.

Flat axe heads are the earliest type of copper-alloy axes used in Britain. During the Bronze Age, flat axe heads were used in much the same way that axes are used today, primarily as a tool. This small flat axe head has the beginnings of a 'stop ridge'. The 'stop' marks a change in technology from simple flat axes to more effective palstaves. The stop ridge allowed the axe to be held more securely within the haft. The patina across most of the axe head has been worn, and localised corrosion has penetrated the surface. This has left much of the axe covered in deep craters or pocks. Newly made, the object would have had a smooth golden surface, both practical to use and impressive to see. This axe is in the Migdale tradition, named after the Bronze Age hoard discovered in Migdale, Sutherland.

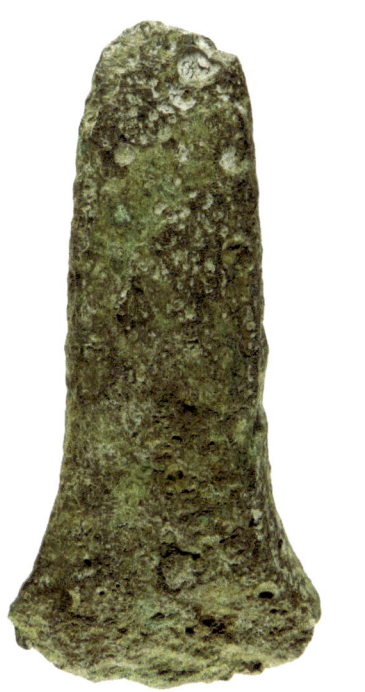
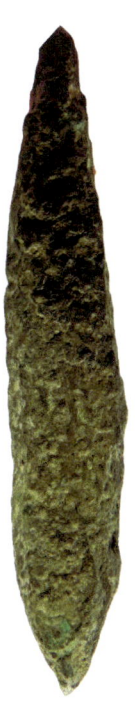
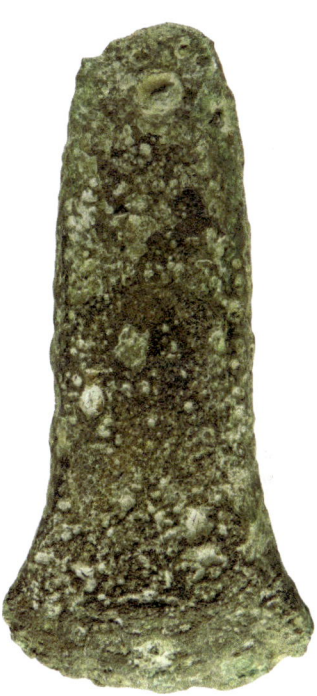

3. Copper-alloy axe (LVPL1357)
Early Bronze Age (1750–1500 BC)
Discovered in Warburton in 2000. Length 61.5 mm.

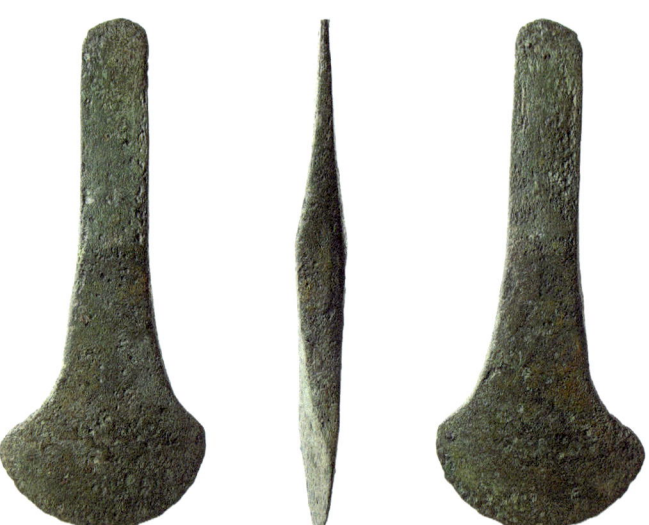

Not all axes are used for chopping down trees. This early Bronze Age developed flat axe is much more likely to have been used as a specialist tool for woodworking. The axe has a narrow body and splayed cutting edge, which is unusual. This 'Arreton' axe is named after a hoard discovered on Arreton Down on the Isle of White before 1735. A high number of Arreton type axes are decorated, which suggests that they had a symbolic status as well as a practical use.

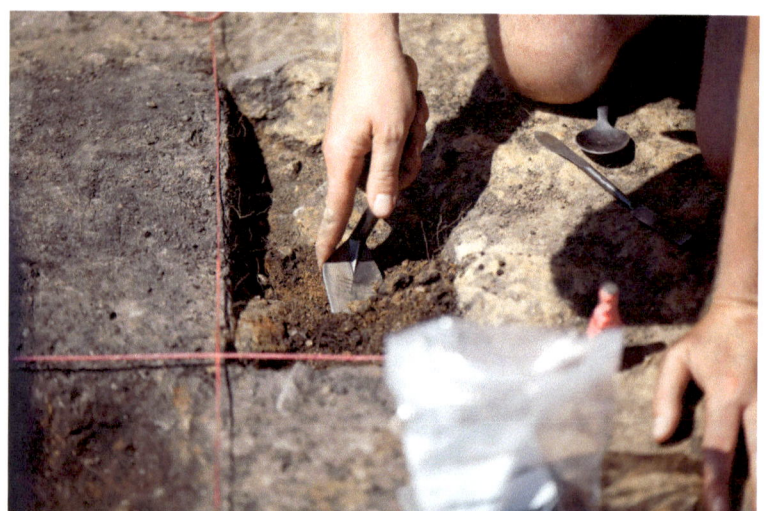

Excavation of a possible prehistoric hearth in the field below Shaw Cairn, Mellor, where similar tools to this chisel would have been familiar to the wearer of the amber necklace discovered in 2008.
(Andy Brown)

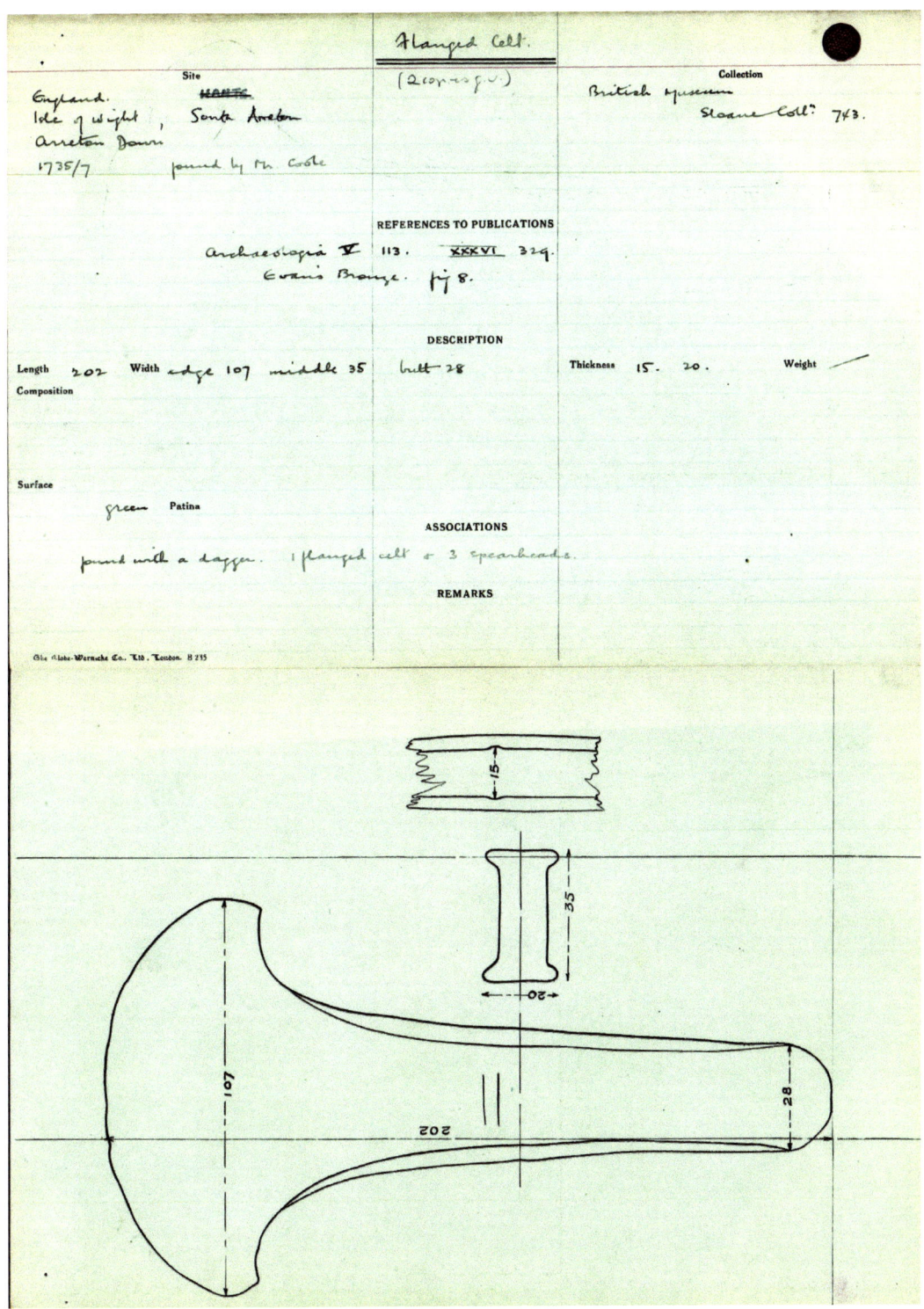

Example of an Arreton Down axe, taken from a British Museum index card for an axe from the Arreton Down Hoard. (Trustees of the British Museum)

4. Copper-alloy palstave axe head (LVPL-C9CBCE)
Early/Middle Bronze Age (1600–1300 BC)
Discovered in 2015 in Heywood. Length 155.19 mm.

Objects are sometimes discovered on metal-detecting 'rallies', where a large group of metal detectorists search the fields together. This was the case with this fantastic palstave axe, which was recorded by the Finds Liaison Officer in attendance. The blade of the palstave is crescent-shaped, with expanding sides and a wide convex cutting edge. The blade is decorated with a central midrib. The palstave has a mid-brown patina, with patches of light green corrosion showing through in places. The axe is un-abraded, showing it has not been moved around in the plough soil from where it was first buried by a stream.

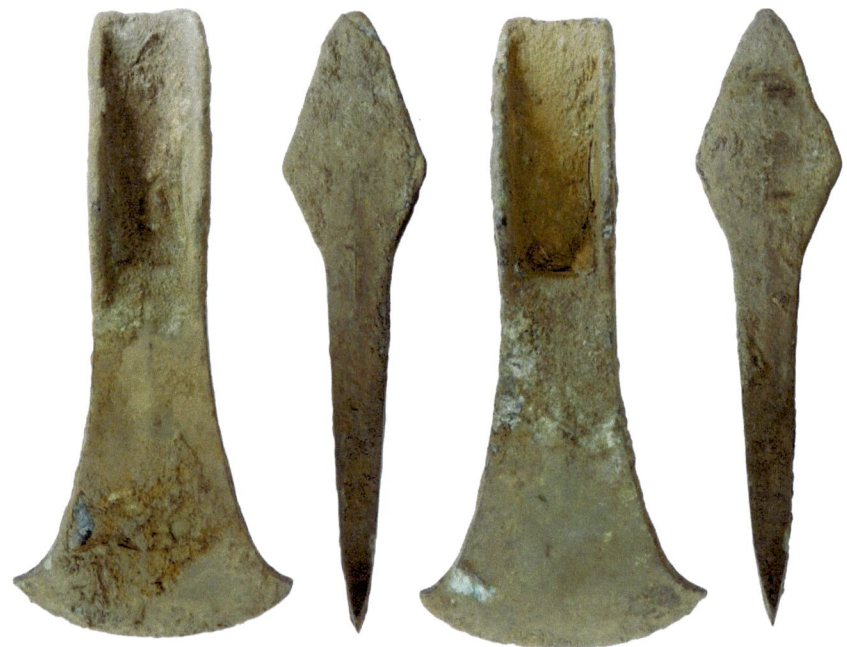

5. Copper-alloy socketed spear head (LVPL1120)
Bronze Age (1400–1300 BC)
Discovered in 1990 in Bury. Length 125 mm.

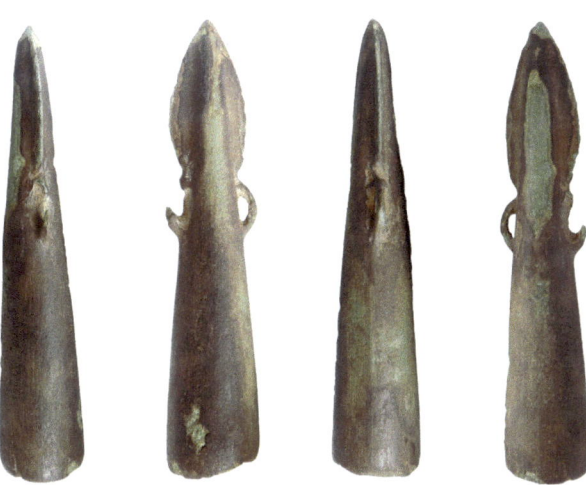

The spearhead has a short, leaf-shaped blade, with a prominent central rib extending to the tip. The socket is substantial, and the wall of the socket varies in thickness. Either side of the object is a side loop, one of which is partly missing. These were used to secure the handle to the spearhead. The object is a typical example from the Taunton metalworking phase, which has strong links with northern France. 599 Bronze Age spearheads have currently been recorded on the PAS database, twenty-nine of which are from the North West, while only two have been recorded from Greater Manchester.

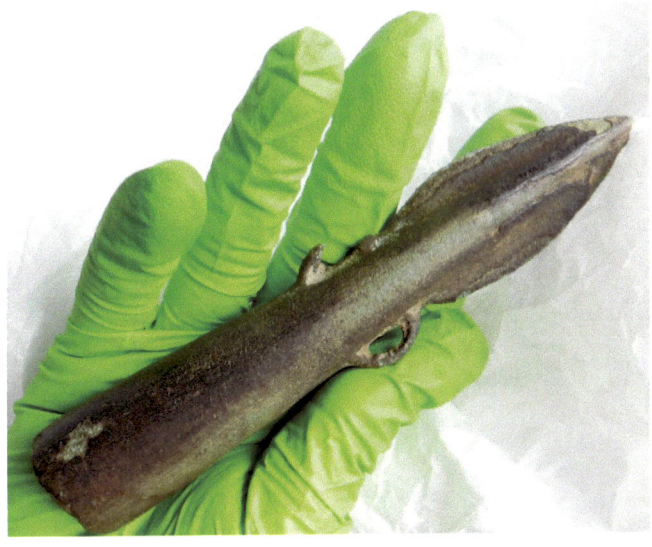

Iron Age (800 BC–AD 42)

6. Copper-alloy figurine (LVPL-904BD3)
Late Iron Age – early Roman (100 BC–AD 100)
Discovered in 2014 in Stockport. Length 46.25 mm.

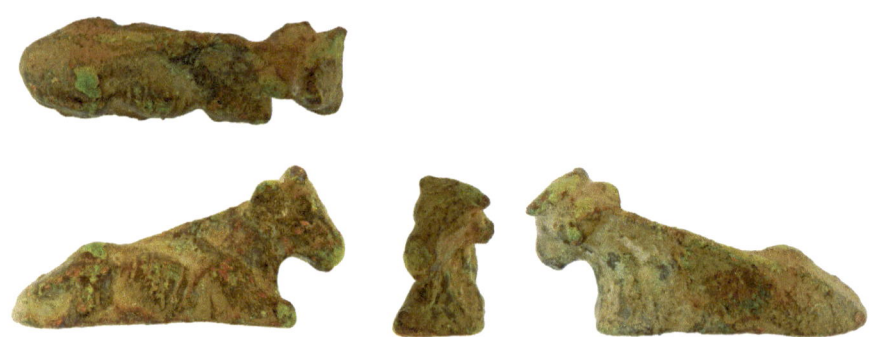

This bull figurine appears to have formed part of a larger artefact such as a vessel. The animal is lying down, with its head slightly turned to one side. The head has ears that project sideways and incomplete horns curving upwards. The incised eyes are lentoid (pointed oval) in shape. Small depressions indicate nostrils and a horizontal groove forms the mouth. The legs of the bull are tucked under the body and the tail curls around the rear and up onto its back. Seven incised lines on one side of the object represent the animal's ribs. Lines running down the nape of the neck indicate hair. The base is flat around the edge with a hollowed centre. This hollow would be filled with solder, so as to fix it onto the rim of a large vessel.

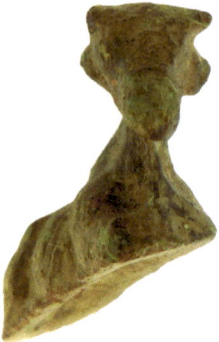

Bulls represent strength and power, and are often seen as sacred. Few bronze bulls are known from Britain and those discovered often decorate buckets, cauldrons and other vessels. This example may have been made in Britain or possibly imported from Roman Gaul.

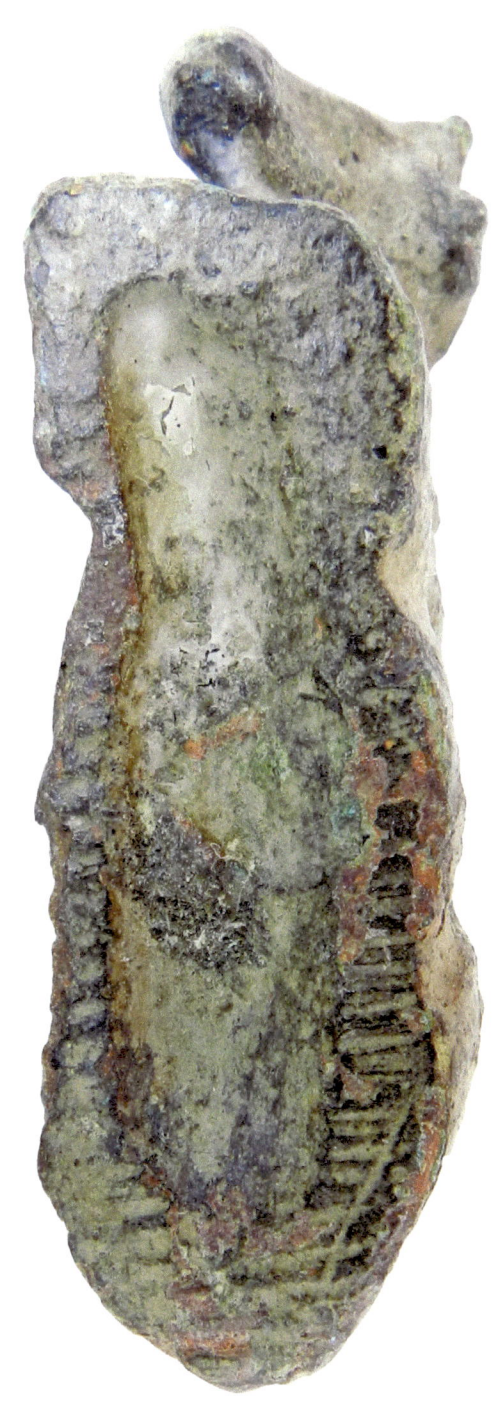

23

7. Iron and copper alloy linch pin (LVPL-DE01E1)
Late Iron Age – early Roman (100 BC–AD 100)
Discovered in 2015 in Stockport. Length 81.09 mm.

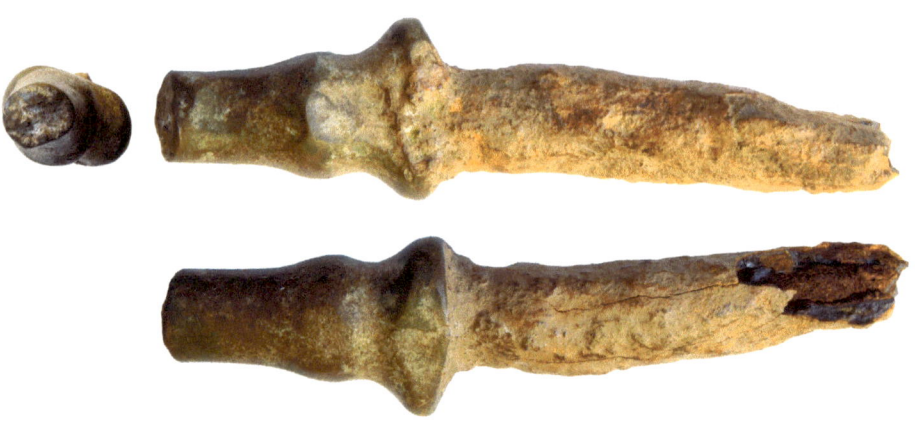

Linch pins are long iron bars used to pin the wheel hub onto the axle of Iron Age chariots. This artefact consists of a circular, sectioned iron shank, surmounted at one end by an incomplete copper-alloy terminal. The broken copper-alloy end of the object would probably have been highly decorated, as in the enamelled example below. The terminal expands outwards with a 'flared skirt', where it joins the iron shaft and has a circumferential collar. The opposite end of the shaft is incomplete and corroded. Many undamaged linch-pin terminals are beautifully decorated. Although we say 'chariots', it is equally possible that it was from a large farm cart.

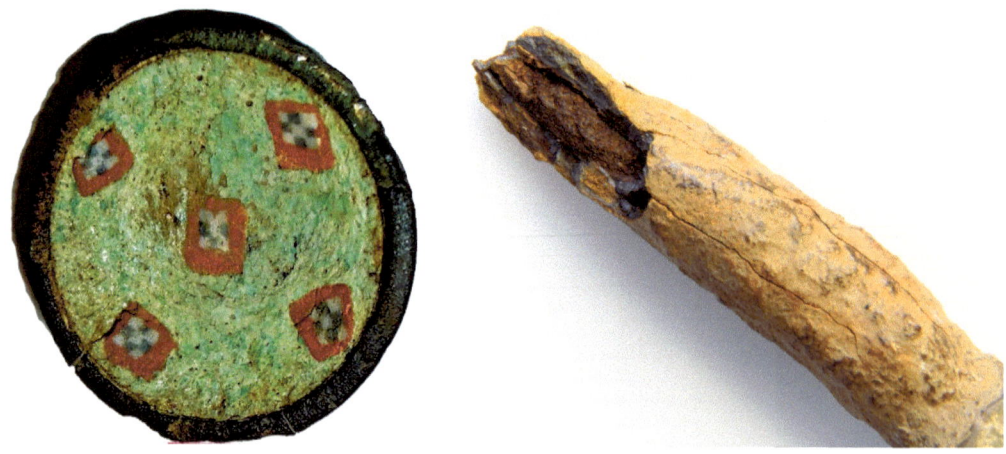

Left: LVPL-951B69: Decorated terminal of an Iron Age – Roman linch pin from North Yorkshire.

8. Copper-alloy stud (LVPL-316F38)
Late Iron Age – early Roman (100 BC–c. AD 120)
Discovered in 2003 in Hale Barns. Diameter 27 mm.

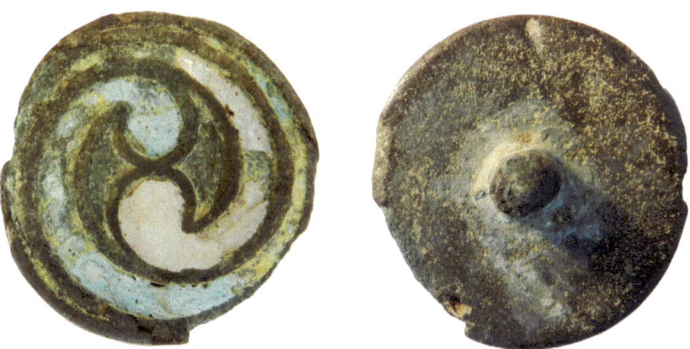

This decorative stud was made in the La Tène style, which was common to metalwork of the late Iron Age and early Roman period. The decoration on the upper surface is made up of two spiralling 'commas', which interlock to form two 'fins'. The 'commas' are infilled with turquoise and white enamel. The raised rim around the edge is now mostly missing. On the back of the circular object is a short central stud for attachment. The Celtic art decorating this object is also known as 'mirror style', due to its similarity to the decoration on Iron Age mirrors. When first made, the copper alloy would have shined bright gold, while the contrasting enamelled cells would draw attention to both the wealth and style of the wearer.

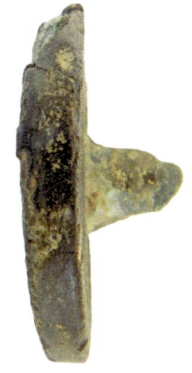

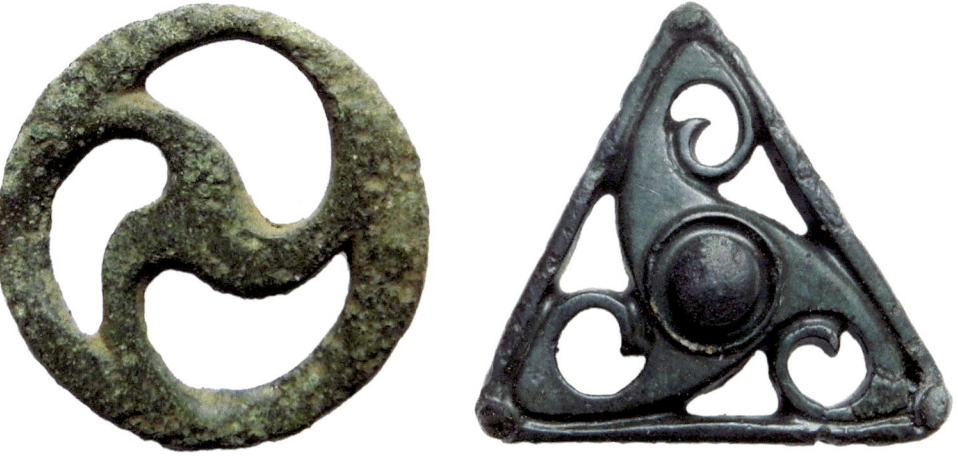

LVPL-DDC778 & LVPL-78F55A: Iron Age fob danglers with similar comma-style decoration.

9. Gold-plated Iron Age stater (LVPL-E309D9)
Iron Age (AD 43-50)
Discovered in 2016 in Trafford. Diameter 19 mm.

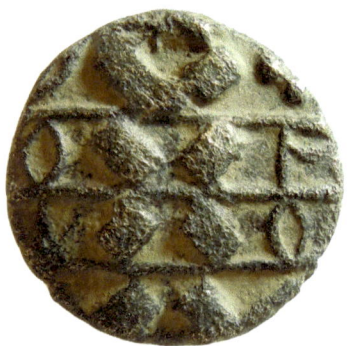 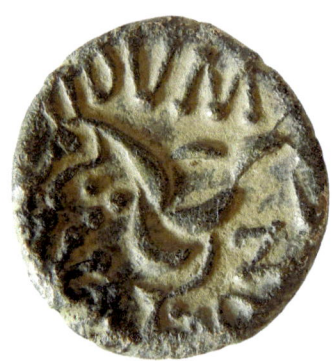

This is one of over 30,000 Iron Age coins that have been found in Britain. It is a contemporary copy of a gold-plated stater with a copper-alloy core. It copies a coin of the North-Eastern region tribe known today as the Corieltavi, whose coinage circulated around the River Humber, North Lincolnshire and Yorkshire. The obverse (front) of the coin depicts a vertical wreath over two lines of inscription between plain lines, reading *'VOLI'* and *'SIOS'*. The reverse depicts a stylised horse facing left, with three pellets below the head and one pellet below tail. It is inscribed with the letters *'DVM'* above, *'NOVE'* below, and *'LLAVNOS'* in front of the horse. This identifies 'Volisios Dumnovellaunos' as the ruler or issuer of this coin type. Volisios and Dumnovellaunos may have been two individuals collaborating to make these coins. Iron Age coins didn't function as money in the way we know it; they were much more than that, representing belonging, allegiance and tribal ties. The fact that this is a copy would not have mattered to the owner – it showed that he belonged to, owed fealty towards or identified with a specific group of people.

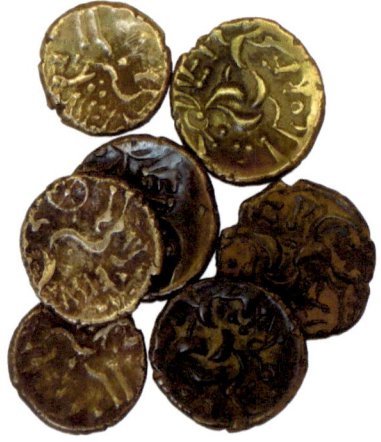

LVPL-DFD9E1: A hoard of similar Iron Age staters found in Cheshire and acquired by the Museum of Liverpool and Congleton Museum MOL2015.51.1-35.

10. Copper alloy harness fitting (LVPL-553944)
Late Iron Age – early Roman (AD 50–AD 250)
Discovered in 2007 in Stockport. Length 19 mm.

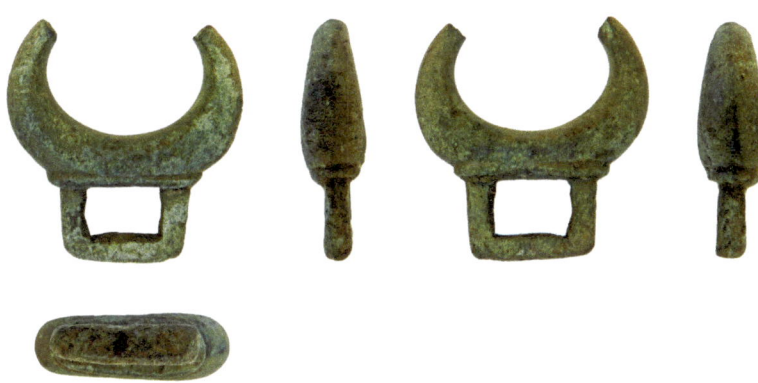

This harness fitting is known as a terret ring or rein-guide and is a dropped bar type. This is a common imported type, manufactured from the mid-first century AD. It is made up of an undecorated oval loop with a sub-rectangular bar cast in one piece. The rectangular loop is set on a moulded oval platform, on the larger loop. The object has broken where the thinnest part of the loop would have been. British chariots were typically drawn by ponies attached with a yoke. Terrets, used in groups of five, were set in line along the yoke in order to guide the rein, preventing them from becoming tangled. This form may have been used by the Roman army on carts and wagons that carried equipment and goods.

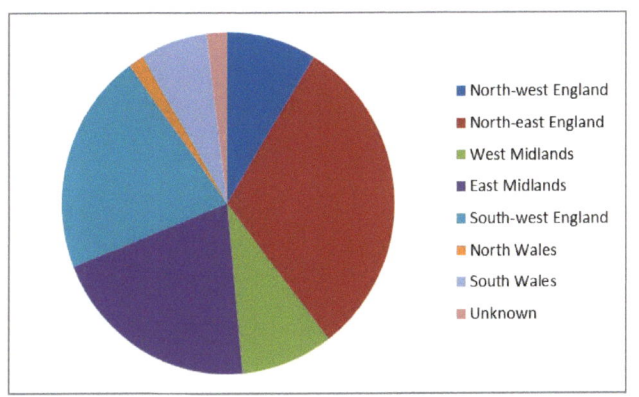
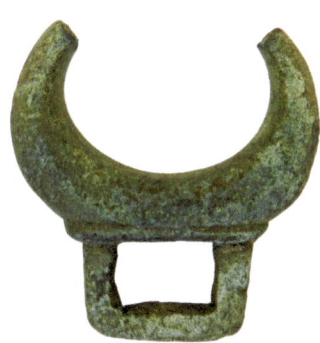

Distribution of terrets in England and Wales. (Dr Anna Lewis)

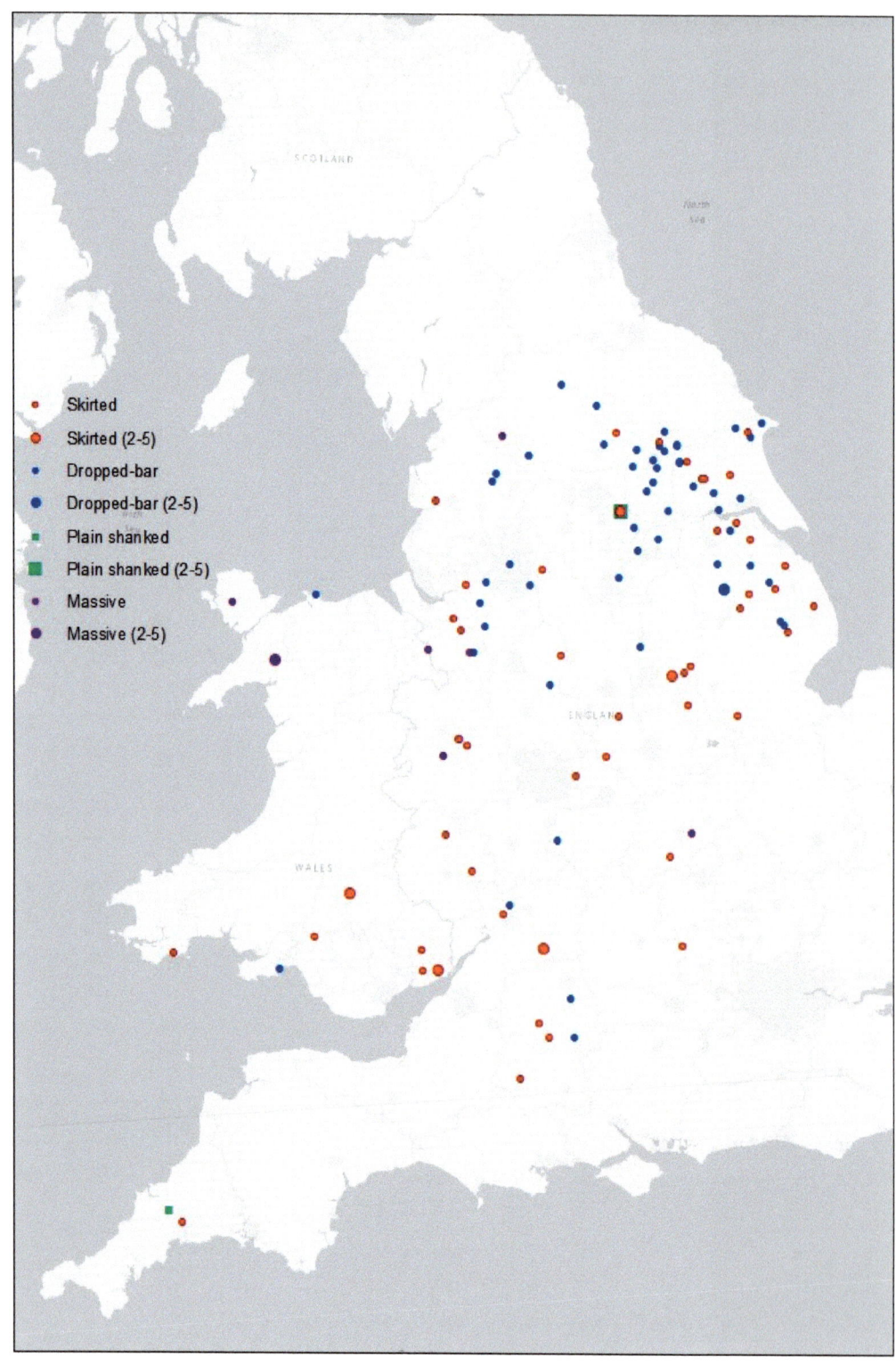

The distribution of different types of terrets and the quantity of types. (Dr Anna Lewis)

Chapter 2
Roman (AD 43–409)

Positioned on the Roman road network, the fort at Manchester (*Mamucium*) formed a key location on the York (*Eboracum*) to Chester (*Deva Victrix*) trans-Pennine route. Within central Manchester in the Castlefield area lie the remains of *Mamucium*, which was probably established by the mid-AD 70s. The fort was garrisoned by auxiliary soldiers whose duty was to guard the road. The presence of the army in this sparsely populated area resulted in the growth of a civilian population. Following the abandonment of the fort, at the end of the fourth century AD the area reverted to agricultural land, and so a build-up of medieval and post-medieval occupation material over the Roman has not occurred. Looking at Manchester today, it is very easy to forget that the city owes its origins to the Romans. However, in places, Roman Manchester is just 5 cm beneath our feet!

Not far from Manchester, another fort and other amenities, such as a large bath house, were established at Wigan (thought to be named *Coccium*). Perhaps the unusual Pannonian brooch below, found in Wigan, belonged to a soldier from the fort – or could it have been dropped by a messenger traveling this important network of Roman roads? Fourteen Roman coin hoards have recently been added to the PAS database as part of a British Museum project, two of which are discussed below. Eight of the fourteen come from

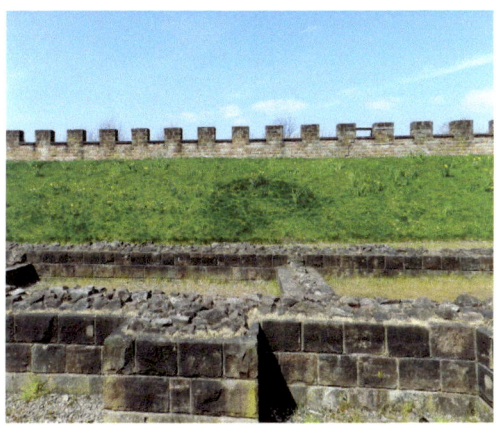
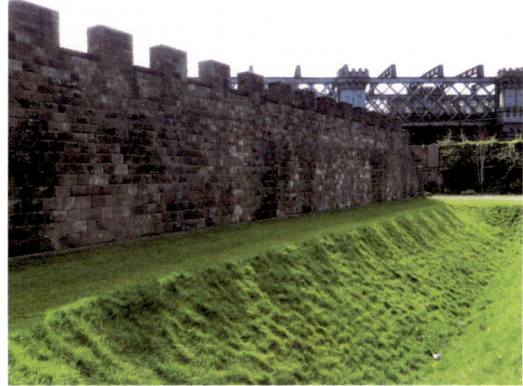

central Manchester, which was clearly a focal point of activity, while one has been recorded from Wigan. Many of these hoards were discovered prior to the existence of PAS and the 1996 Treasure Act, and much of the information (and in some cases finds) has been lost or dispersed.

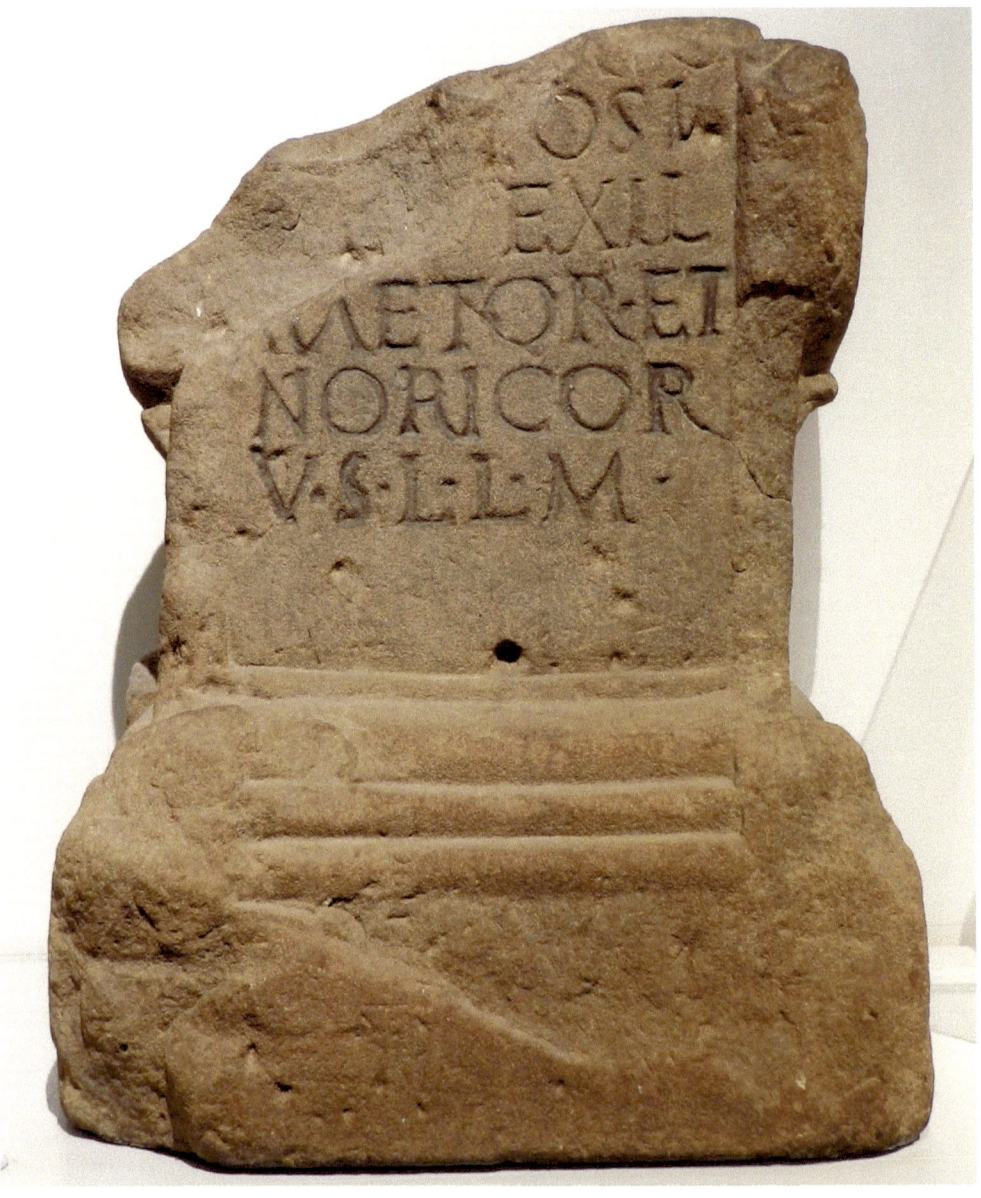

Roman altar set up by commander in charge of a temporary task force of soldiers from Austria and Switzerland, found in Castlefield. (Manchester Art Gallery)

11. The Warburton hoard: Silver republican denarii (LVPL-3C5036/2010-T465)
Roman (130 BC–AD 9)
Discovered in 2010 in Warburton; acquired by Manchester Museum.

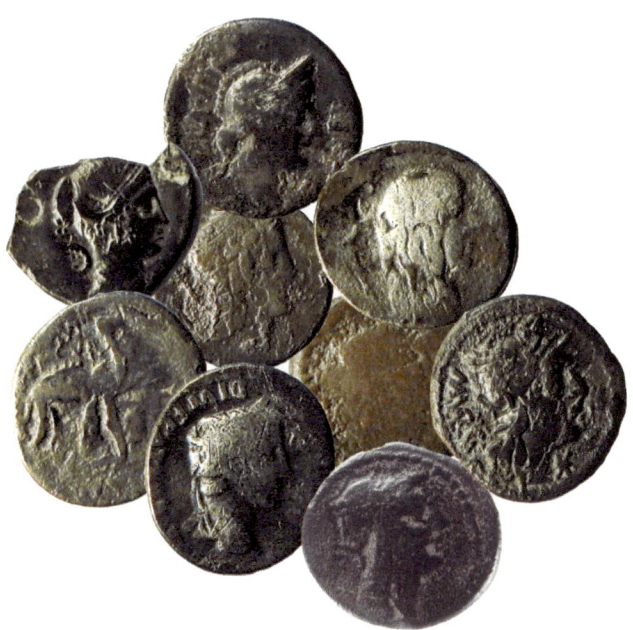

The Warburton hoard contains nine silver denarii. Most of the coins were made in the republican period (between 130 and 48 BC), and would probably have come to Britain during the Claudian invasion of AD 43. These coins were made / minted in Rome, and show the names of the various junior magistrates responsible for their production. The latest coin was minted in Lyons (France) for Augustus, the first emperor of Rome, between 2 BC and AD 9. We can probably connect its arrival with military activity of some kind – perhaps the lost purse of a soldier, passing through the area. What we do know is that the coins are of a very good silver and were in circulation for a long time before they were buried. These early coins are seldom found in the North West.

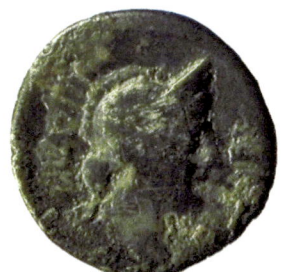 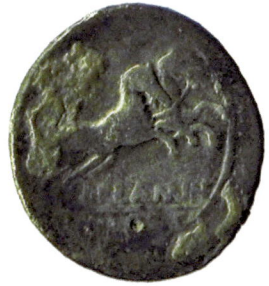

Republican denarius, Moneyer: Flaminius Chilo, L 109–108 BC.

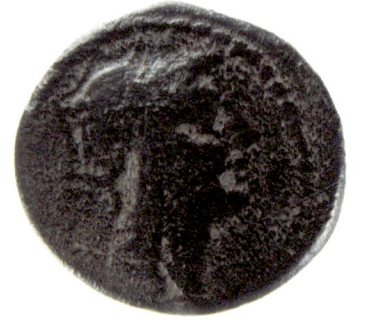 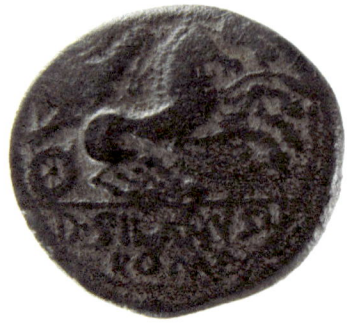

A denarius of Decimus Junius Silanus of 91 BC.

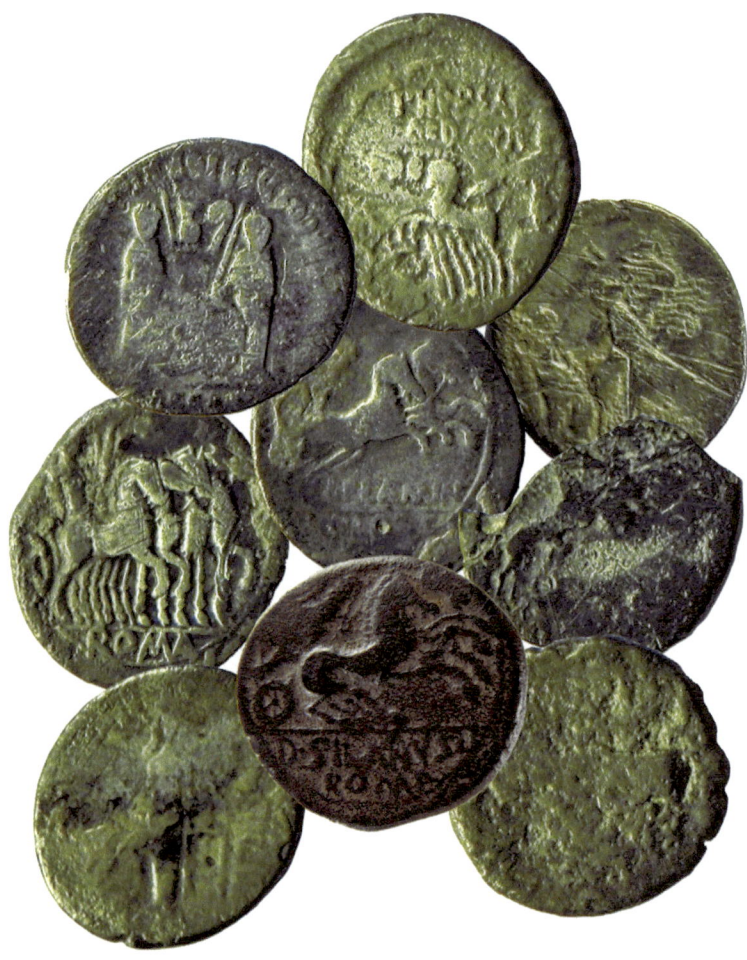

Reverse sides of the Warburton hoard coins.

12. Silver zoomorphic bracelet (LVPL-D33064/2005 T566)
Roman (AD 43–410)
Discovered in 2005 in Trafford and acquired by Manchester Museum. Length 148 mm.

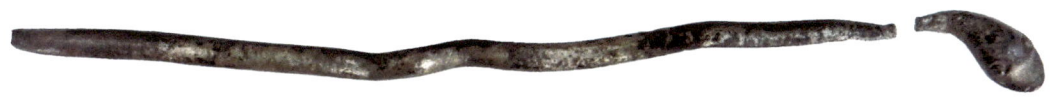

This bracelet, pulled straight in antiquity, consists of a narrow strip of silver with a rounded zoomorphic terminal shaped as a snake's head; this has become detached. Originally the opposite end of the bracelet probably had a similar snake head, which is now lost. The snake's mouth is open and its eyes are formed from raised pellets on each side of the head. The top of the head has been pierced by a single drilled hole. Evidence at the other end of the bracelet suggests that it has broken at the point where another hole had been drilled. These possible fixing holes, combined with the straightening of the bracelet, suggest the object was reused to form a mount or a binding strip.

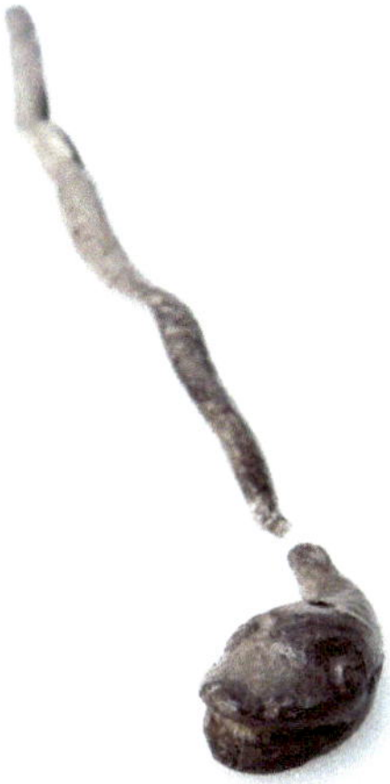

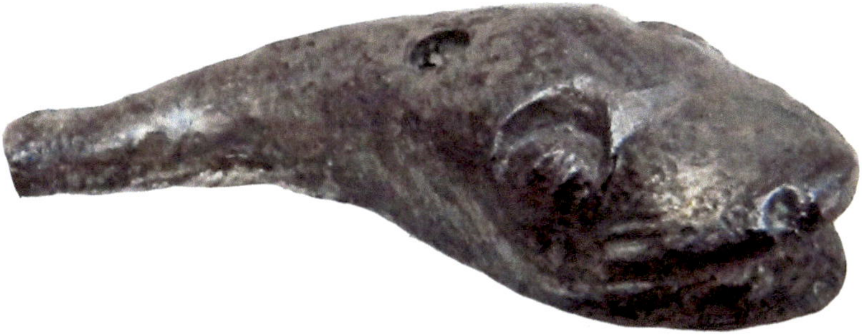

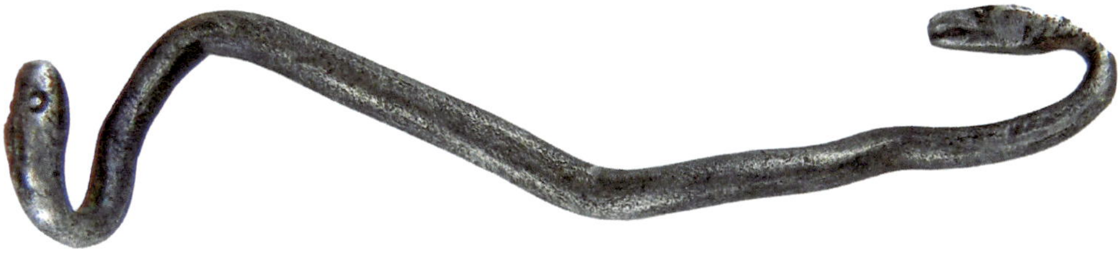

LVPL-D7FD21: This similar but smaller snake-shaped finger ring from Nottinghamshire has also been unravelled.

13. Copper-alloy *Kraftig Profilierte* type brooch (LVPL-1B0623)
Roman (AD 43–100)
Discovered in 2007 in Wigan and donated to the PAS handling collection. Length 40 mm.

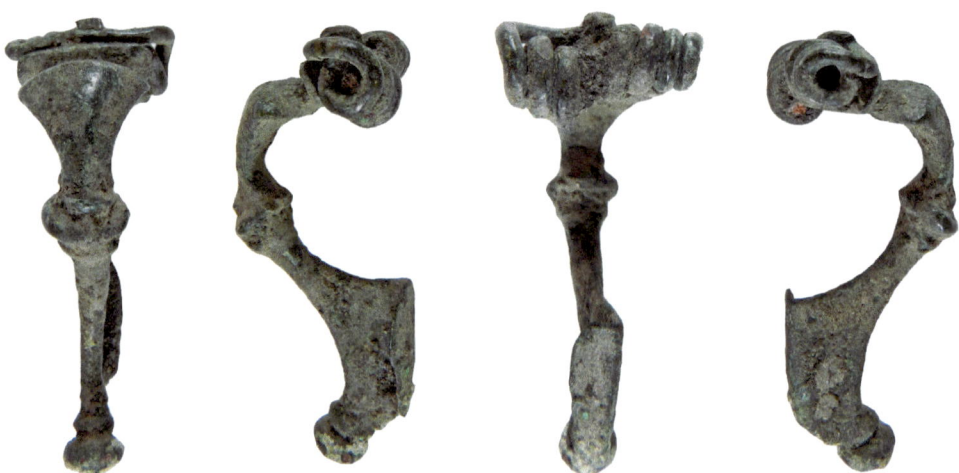

Kraftig Profilierte brooches come from Pannonia, an area on the Danube–Rhine frontier in Germany. Brooches of this type are believed to have been brought to Britannia by the Ninth Legion, which was drafted from Pannonia in AD 43. These brooches are most commonly found in the south and east of England than the west, so this find is especially important. The brooch is complete, apart from its missing pin. The spring has been formed by a single length of copper alloy wire being turned to form a spring of six coils with an external cord. The pin is lost. The bow is arched, with a pronounced decorative moulding at its centre. The broad head does not cover the spring, which is held in place by a forward hook. There is a single terminal knob at the foot, which has a collar. The catch plate, which would have secured the pin, is complete.

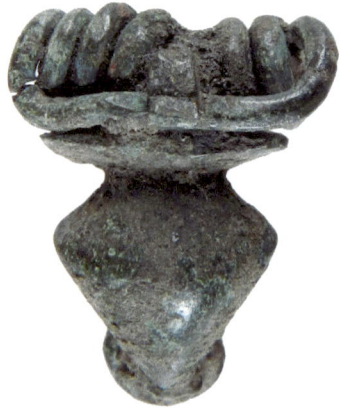

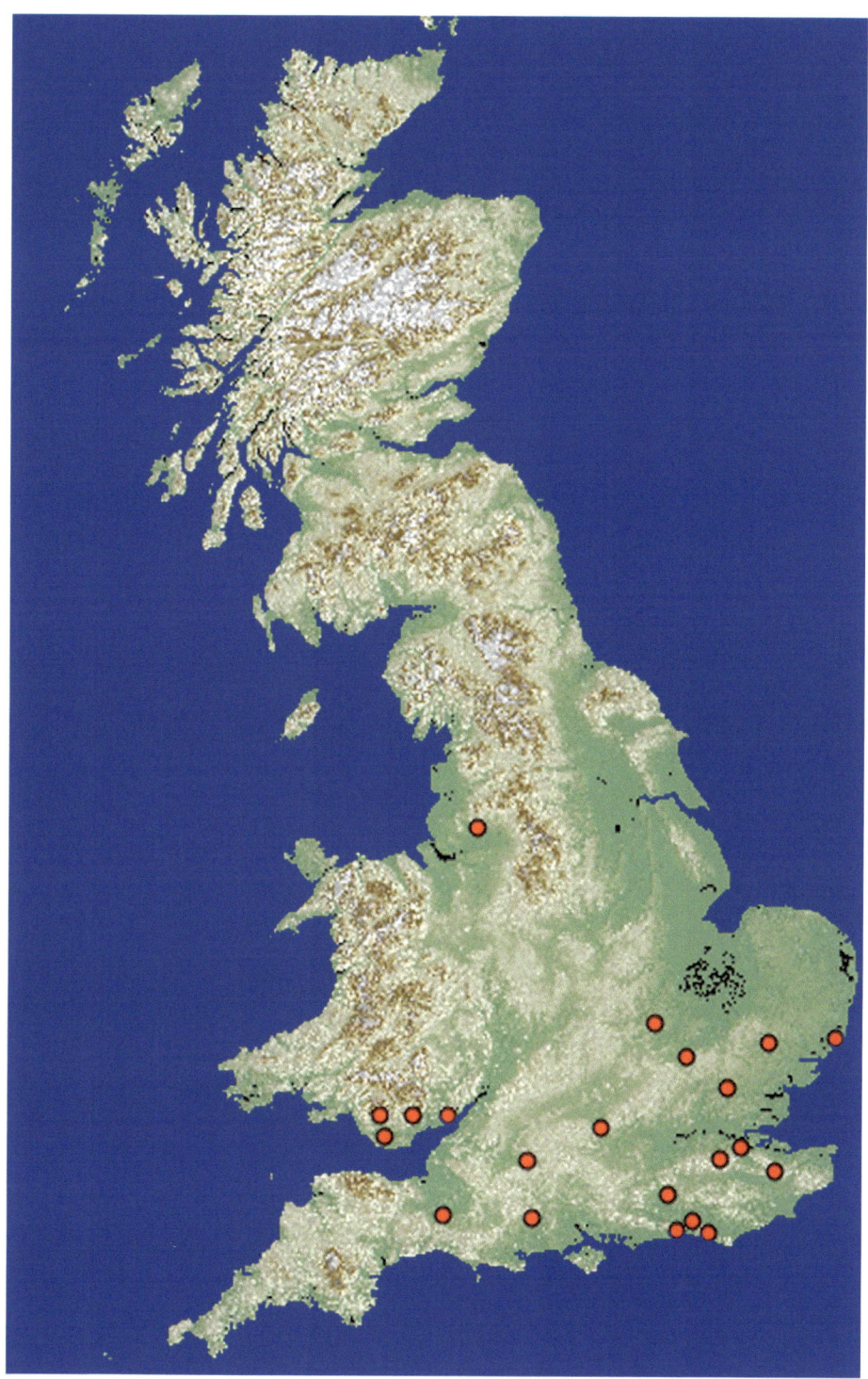

Distribution of *Kraftig Profilierte* brooches recorded on the Portable Antiquities Scheme database to date. Map kindly provided by Peter Reavill. (Contains OS data © Crown copyright [and PAS database right], 2016)

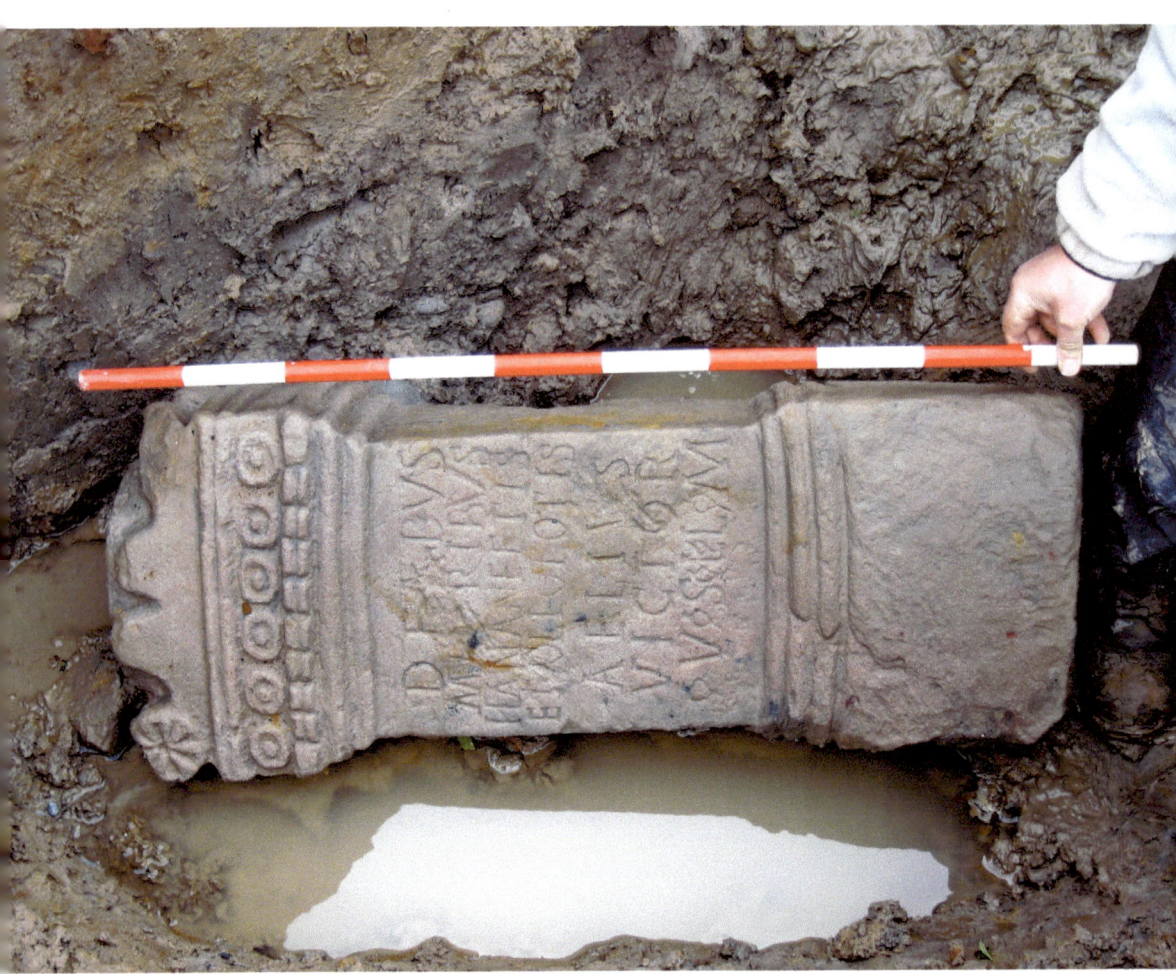

Roman altar discovered during excavation in 2008 from Chester Road in Roman Manchester (now in Manchester Museum). This altar is inscribed with the name 'Aelius Victor', the second named Roman from Manchester. Aelius Victor erected the altar in the honour of Cannanefates, the mother goddess of a Germanic tribe. (Norman Redhead)

14 Copper-alloy coin hoard – the Boothsbank hoard (IARCH-E4F088)
Roman (*c.* AD 293–296)
Discovered in 1989 in Salford; acquired by Salford Museum and Art Gallery.

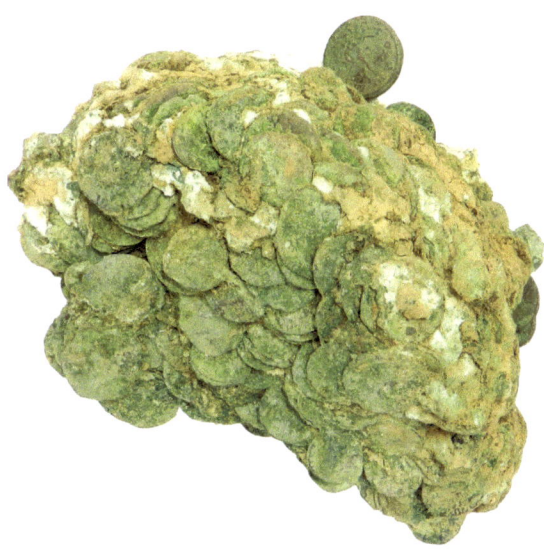

The Boothsbank hoard was discovered in March 1989 during building works in Salford. The hoard consists of several fused, concreted and corroded clumps of copper-alloy 'radiate' coins as well as a number of single loose coins. Due to the condition of the hoard, many of the coins have not been individually counted or identified. Among those that have are a considerable number of coins of the Emperor Allectus (AD 293–296) along with pre-reform radiates of the emperor Diocletian (AD 284–305). Following its discovery, the hoard was professionally excavated by Greater Manchester Archaeological Unit. It is thought that, during the late third century, millions of radiate-style coins were struck every week in mints in Germany and Gaul.

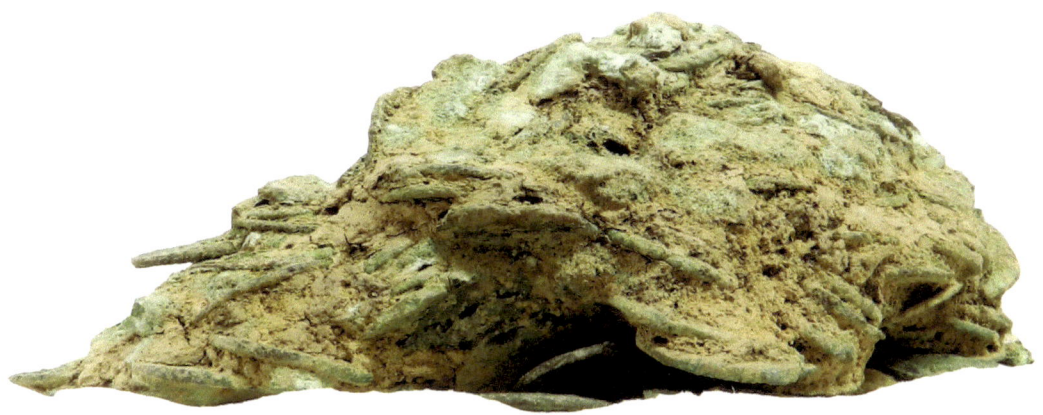

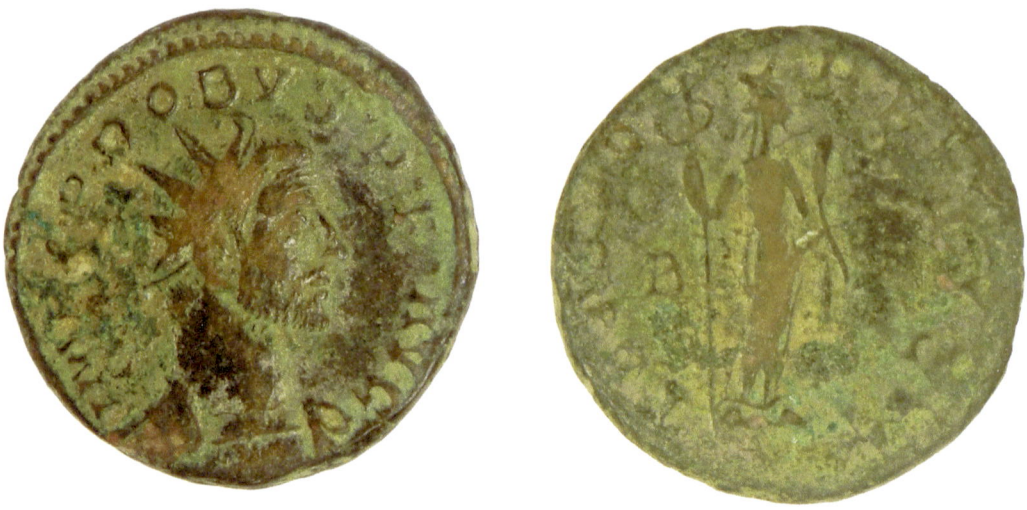

A radiate from the Boothsbank hoard of Marcus Aurelius Probus, born in AD 232. The coin was minted in Lugdunum (modern Lyon, France).

Chapter 3
Early Medieval (AD 410–1066)

There is little evidence of early medieval activity in either the documentary or archaeological sources in the Greater Manchester area. However, we do have some stunning fragments of sculpture, one of which acts as both an archaeological and documentary source. These stone artefacts were discovered on a farm in Milnrow, one built into a wall and the other into the farmhouse itself. One of the most significant factors in looking at ancient sculpture is that, due to their form and weight, most sculptures do not move far from their original locations. Sculpture can, therefore, provide a fairly accurate picture of what was happening during the past, particularly in terms of beliefs. These small fragments are more portable than other forms of sculpture of similar date, such as complete crosses or 'hogback' tombstones. However the 'robbing out' or re-use of old stone usually occurs locally, simply due to convenience and opportunity.

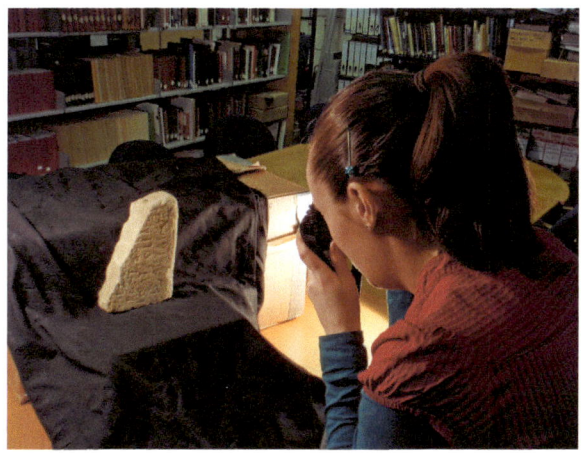
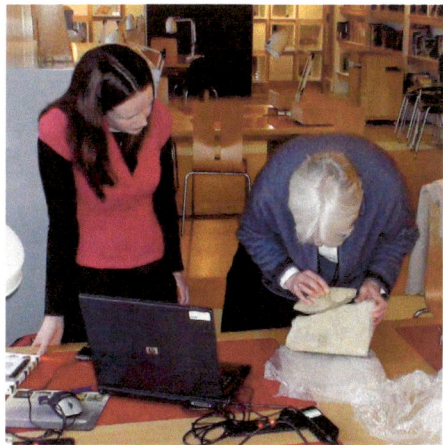

Left: V. Oakden photographing the Milnrow Memorial stone at the Museum of Liverpool.

Right: V. Oakden and Professor Elisabeth Okasha, acting director of the Language Centre, University College Cork, examining the stones in Manchester Museum.

15. Sculpture (LVPL-018000)
Early Medieval (AD 800–1200)
Discovered in 1986/87 in Milnrow. Height 150.5 mm.

This inscribed stone was found built into a doorway of a farm house. One face carries an inscription written in Latin script. Most of the left face of the stone has been cut away and the remains of mortar can be seen where it was built into the doorway. The right side of the stone is decorated with a boss. The script, known as Anglo-Saxon capitals, has been translated by Dr Elisabeth Okasha; it reads:

- sola [-] res [i] eis [-] beata olin q [-e]s avt [a- +]

Tentatively this can be translated as:

'[-] alone [-] by/with these things [-] blessed Olin and [-] or [- +]'.

Olin may be a female name, and this interpretation of the inscription suggests that the stone was once part of a much larger memorial.

Another example is LVPL-01F601; this stone sculpture dates to AD 900–1000. It is carved in relief on both main faces in the form of a hammer-head cross. The arms are defined by

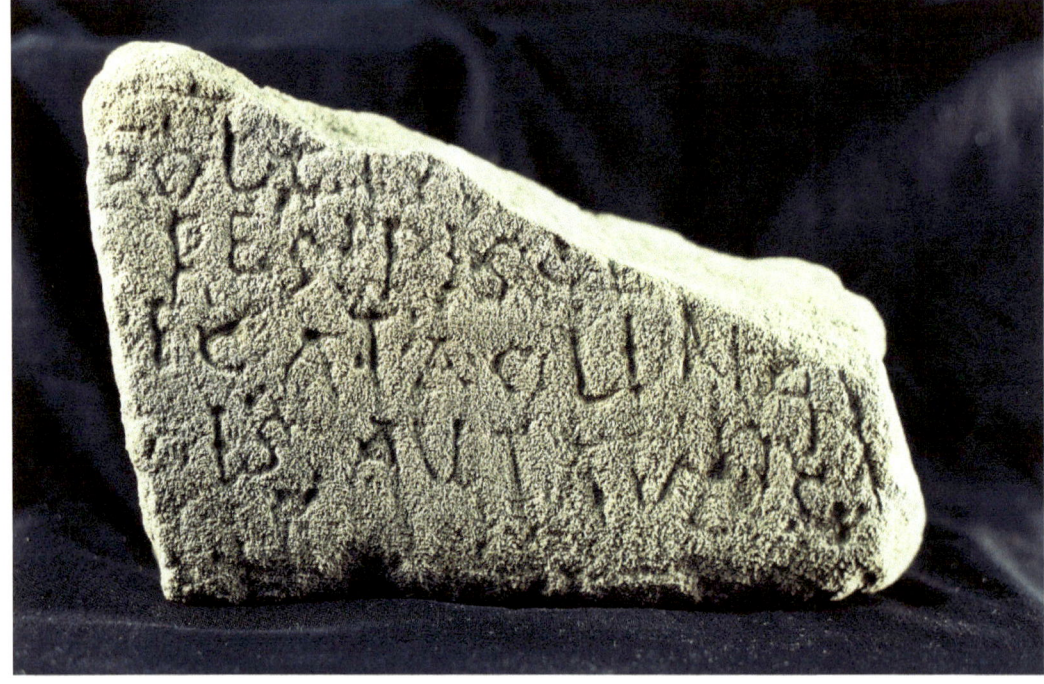

(Copyright Ross Trench-Jellicoe. Reproduced with kind permission)

an edge moulding, within which are worn traces of tightly packed interlace (often found decorating Viking metalwork) formed from interlocking strands. The stone could have been a small disc-headed grave marker or part of a taller circle headed cross. It can be dated to the Viking period from the tenth to the eleventh century.

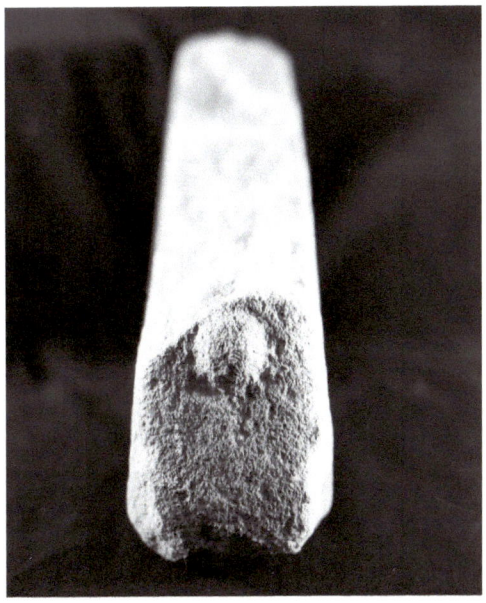

Right: (Copyright Ross Trench-Jellicoe. Reproduced with kind permission)

Below: (Copyright Ross Trench-Jellicoe. Reproduced with kind permission)

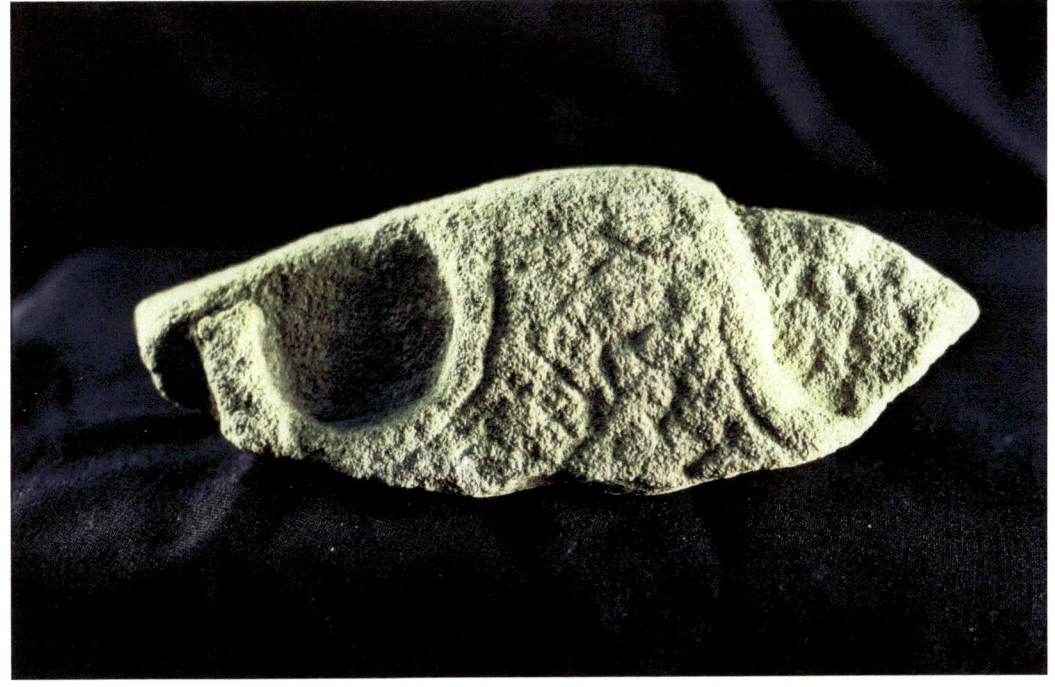

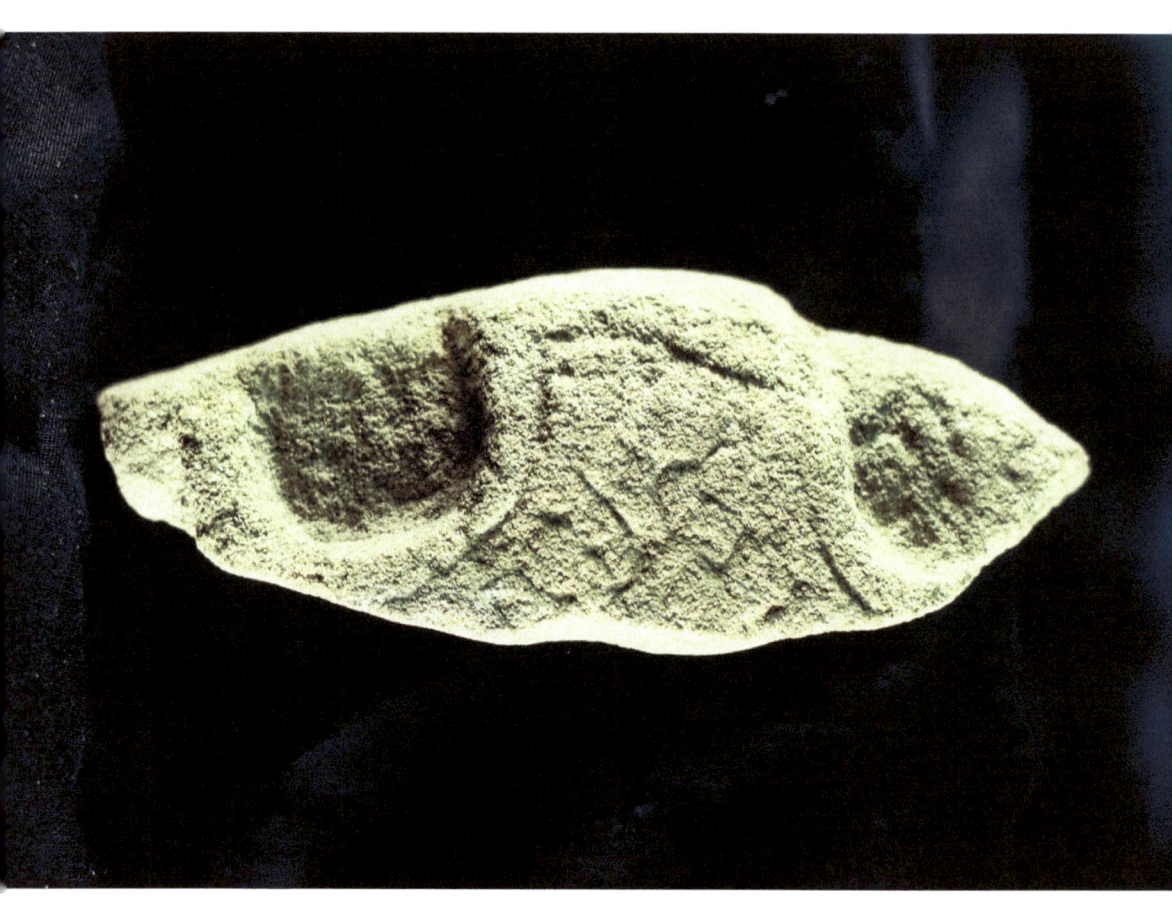

(Copyright Ross Trench-Jellicoe. Reproduced with kind permission)

16. Copper alloy brooch (LVPL-7EBD4F)
Early Medieval (AD 800–1000)
Discovered pre or during 1964 in Bolton. Diameter 70.7 mm.

This bronze penannular brooch, used to fasten clothing, was discovered by a ploughman working the fields near Bolton. Following its discovery, it was sold to a friend of the finder and then to Birmingham Museum in 1964. The brooch is complete and the pin is undecorated. The ring loop of the pin is ribbed with expanded openings. The terminals of the ring expand and are flattened. Between the flattened terminals and the ring are stylised horses' heads. Just sixty-four penannular brooches have been recorded on the PAS database, four of which, including this example, were found in the North West.

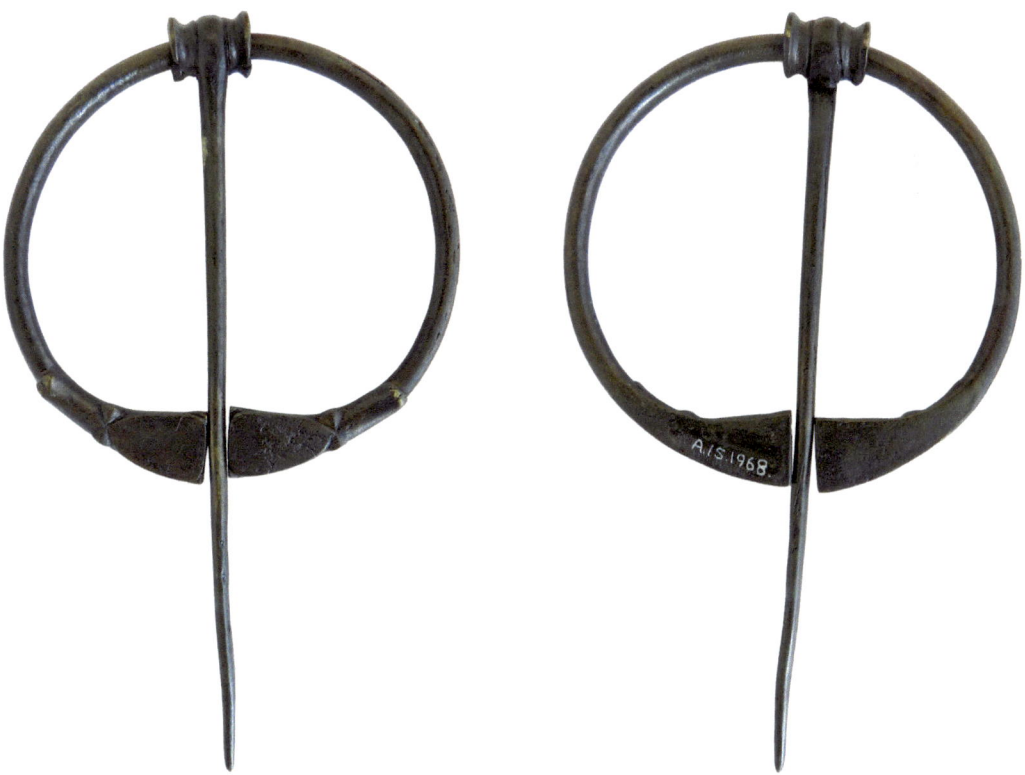

Images of the replica made for Bolton Library & Museums service.

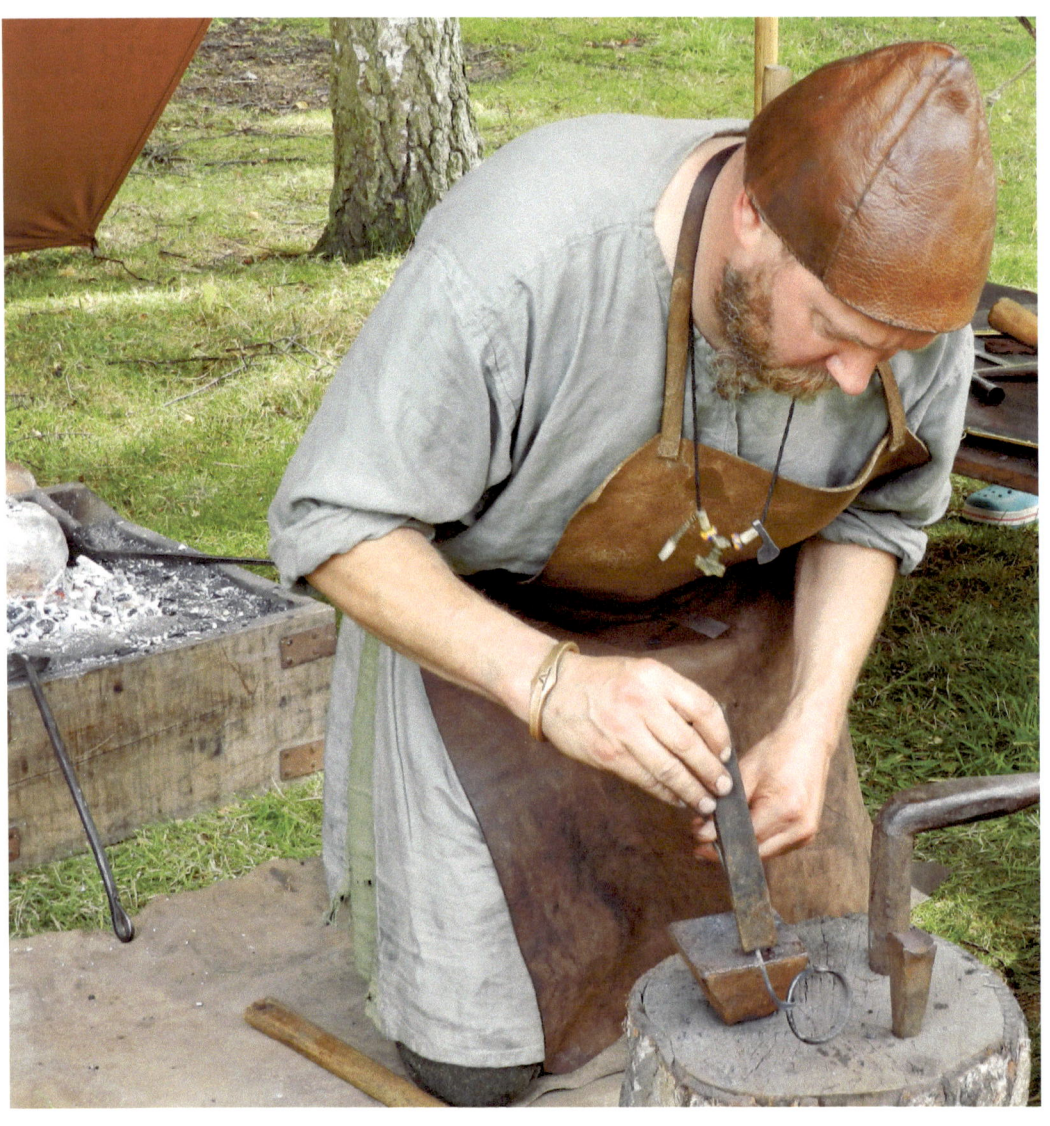

Reenactor making a penannular brooch at Tatton Park.

Chapter 4
Medieval (1066–1539)

The landscape around Manchester was predominantly agricultural during the medieval period and administratively was part of the Salford Hundred, as mentioned in the Domesday Book. The Domesday Book states that 'the Church of St Mary and the Church of St Michael held in Manchester 1 carucate [AN: medieval unit of land] of land quit [exempt] of every customary due except geld [AN: tax assessed on the number of hides]'.

Manchester, now a built-up city, provides little opportunity for chance (un-excavated) finds, and currently just seventy-five medieval objects have been voluntarily recorded on the PAS database.

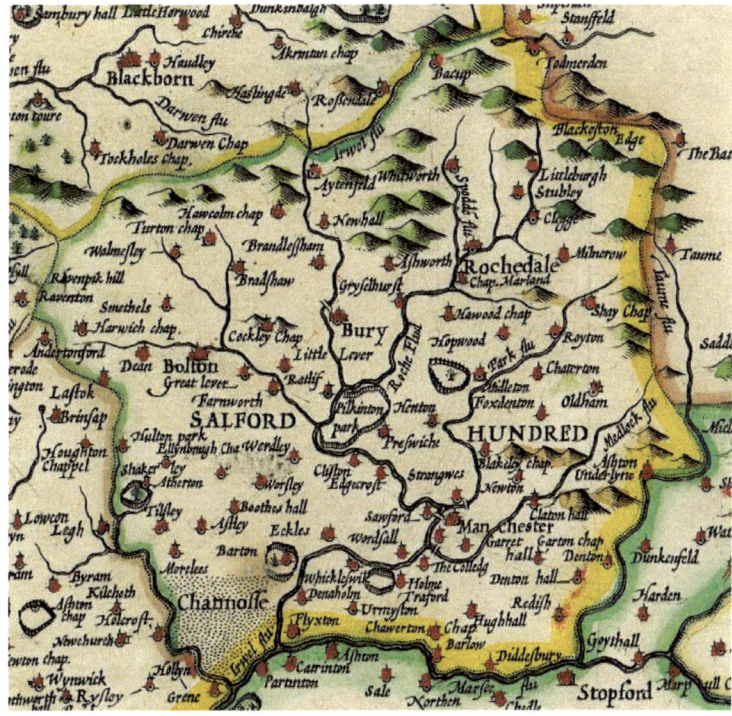

John Speed's map of Lancashire (1610).

17 Silver coin hoard (LVPL-E8761C)
Medieval (AD 1100–1150)
Discovered in 1972 in Prestwich.

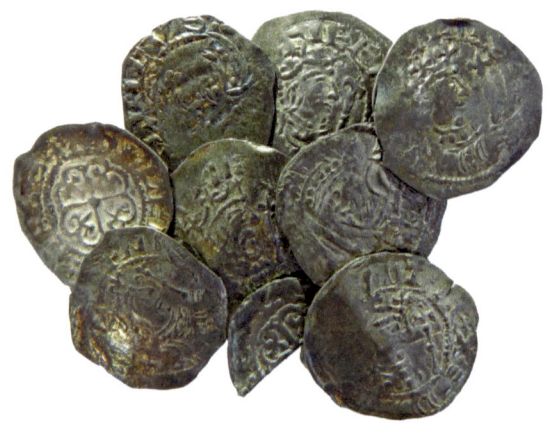

This coin hoard contains 1,065 silver coins of twelfth-century date. The majority were made in the reigns of Henry I (AD 1100–1135) and Stephen (AD 1135–1154). The hoard was found in 1972, during resurfacing work in a Prestwich school playground. This prompted an excavation, which took place between April and October. The excavation found that the coins had been hidden in a container, which was unfortunately broken during the recovery. As with many hoards of the time, the Prestwich hoard was divided up by the finders. 334 were sold in auction by Sotheby's in 1974 with the remainder being split between the Bury, Bolton and British museums.

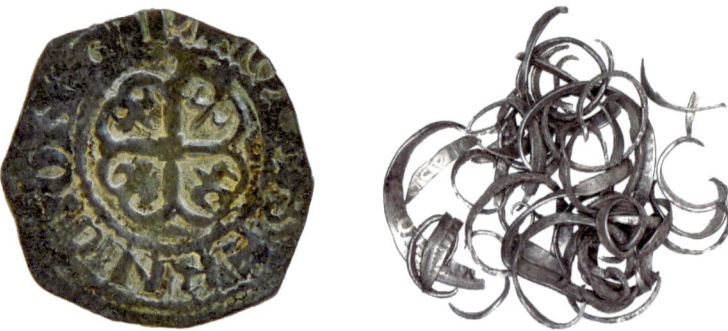

Left: Coin clipping: Medieval coinage was worth its physical weight in silver. As such, small pieces of silver have been clipped (cut) off the edges of these coins. This defacement was illegal but it occurred throughout the period.

Right: DENO-789371: Post-Medieval coin clippings from Derbyshire. (The Portable Antiquities Scheme)

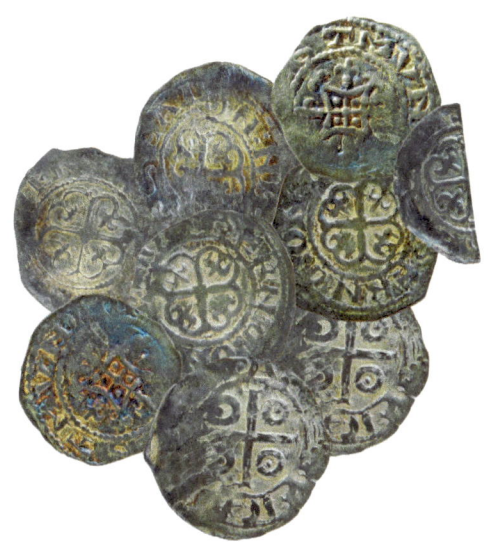

Reverse sides of the Prestwich coins in Bolton Museum.

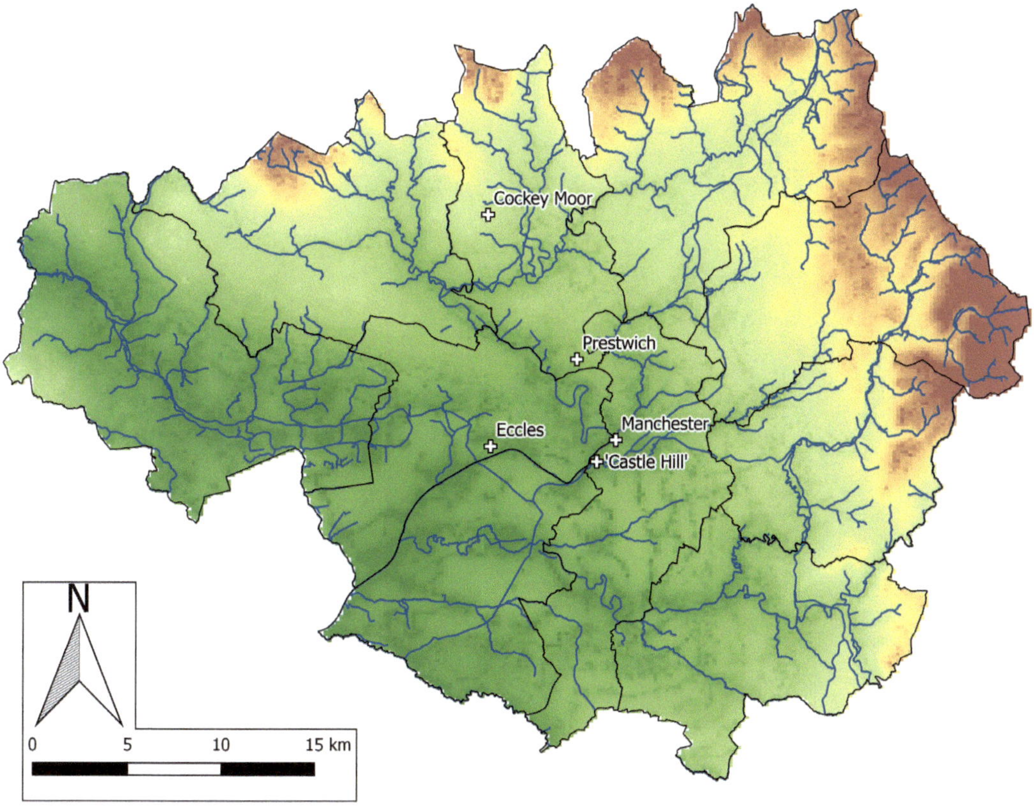

Map showing all of the medieval hoards discovered in Greater Manchester. (Murray Andrews. Contains OS data © Crown copyright [and PAS database right], 2016)

18. Copper-alloy harness pendant (LVPL1797)
Medieval (AD 1200–1400)
Discovered in 2000 in Warburton. Length 57 mm.

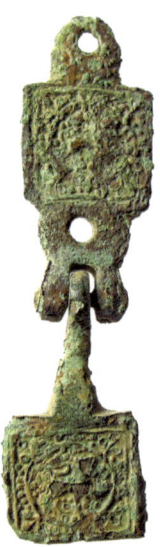

This harness pendant is highly unusual – it comprises a square-shaped suspended pendant and a strap mount. The lower pendant is decorated with a four-legged animal, enclosed within a circular border, while on the external edge are small fleur-de-lis in each corner. The mount is of a square shape in plan, and the decoration echoes the lower design. The mount would have attached to the harness. Traces of the gilding that would have covered this object remain on the outer face. Before being lost to the earth, it would have glinted in the sunshine, offering both a warning that a rider was approaching and a clue as to his identity.

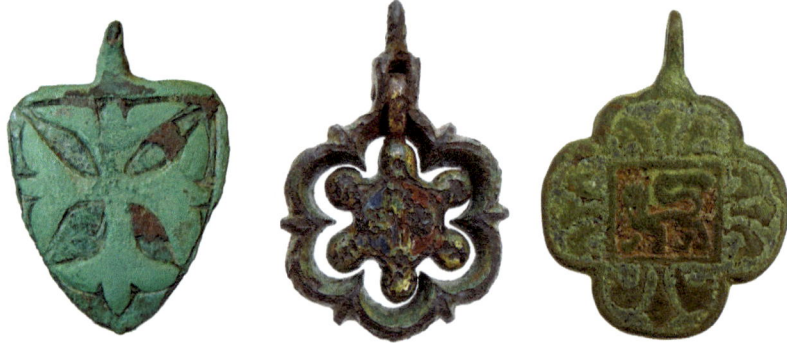

Harness pendants come in a variety of forms, with many displaying the heraldry of those to whom they belonged.

19. Lead-alloy pilgrim's badge (LVPL-8EEAAD)
Medieval to Early Post-Medieval (AD 1200–1550)
Discovered in 2013 in Trafford. Length 27 mm.

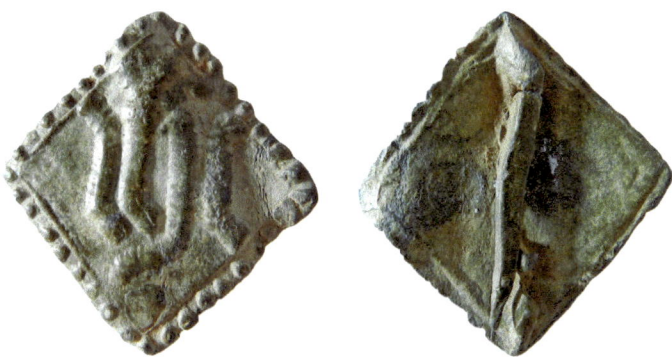

The act of pilgrimage was a central act of worship for all levels of society within the medieval world. Any member or rank of society could undertake pilgrimage and, for those tied to working on the land, it enabled a level of freedom not usually experienced under their feudal overlord. Therefore, pilgrim's badges were important souvenirs that spoke to others of the wearer's faith, determination and, on a more practical level, the fact that they had not been absent from work for no reason. In the centre of this badge are the letters 'IHS' in Gothic script, contained within a beaded border. The initials 'IHS' are a Christogram representing the Latin for 'Jesus the Saviour of Man', *Iesus Hominum Salvator*. Unusually, both the pin and the catch plate, vulnerable to the turn of the plough, survive on the rear of this example.

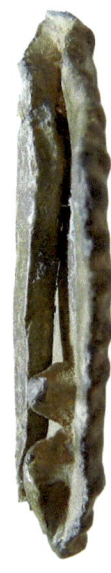

20. Gold and gem brooch (LVPL-039CF2) Accession no. 1977.168, Manchester Art Gallery
Medieval (AD 1280–1320)
Discovered in 1971 in Victoria Street, Manchester. Diameter 40.5 mm.

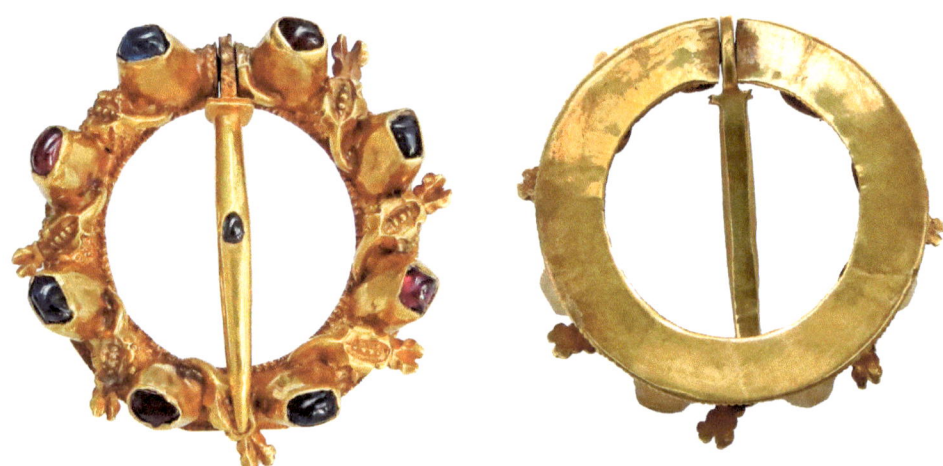

The Victoria Street brooch was discovered by a Salford school teacher during a lunchtime stroll in 1971. It was spotted lying upcast of a North Western Electricity Board trench. The annular brooch is circular in plan and has eight raised collets, equally spaced around the frame. Each collet contains a rounded cabochon (polished and pebble-like) stone setting of alternating garnets and sapphires. Between the collets are open fruit pods with seeds within and the remains of the dried / spent flower. The tip of the pin sits within one of these pods and is itself set with a sapphire cabochon at the mid-point. The pod may represent the fruit of the broom (*Genista sagittalis*), which is thought to have been adopted as a badge by Henry II's father, Geoffrey of Anjou. The brooch, which is of the highest quality of workmanship, was probably made in France.

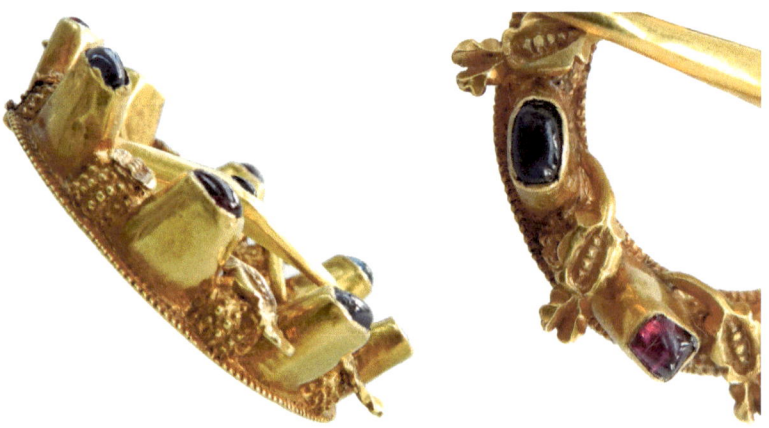

Purchased by Manchester Art Gallery with the assistance of the Victoria & Albert Purchase Grant Fund.

21. Copper-alloy harness stud/mount (LVPL-A90615)
Medieval to Early Post-Medieval (AD 1300–1400)
Discovered in 2015 in Trafford. Length 33 mm.

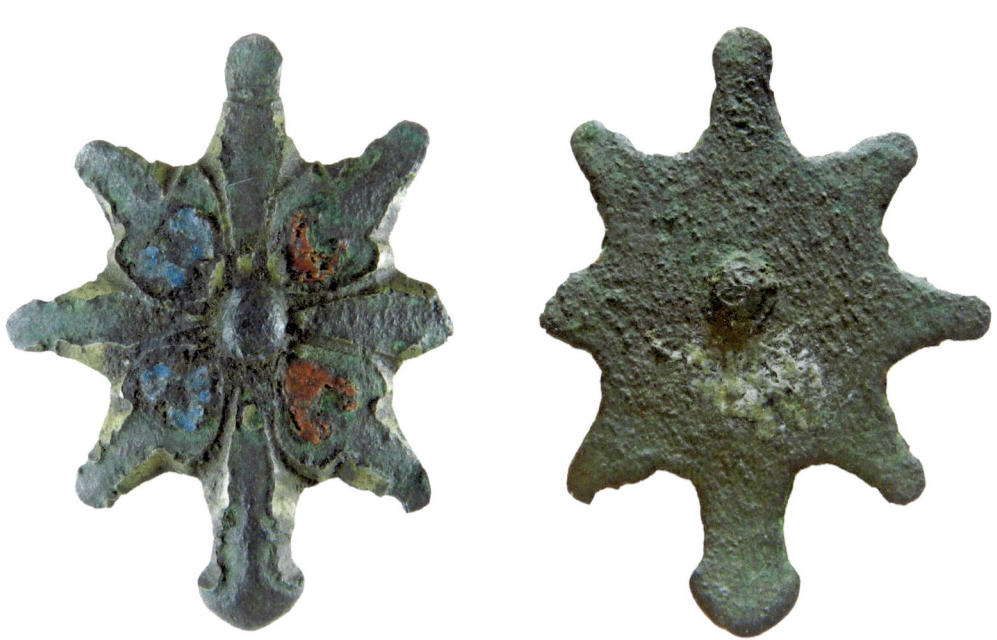

Medieval horses were often heavily decorated with studs and pendants like LVPL1797. These were designed to impress, intimidate and, in the case of heraldic harness fittings, to identify. This incomplete harness stud has seven rounded projections and one longer projection, with a *pelta* or scallop-shaped terminal. In the centre of the object is a domed rivet. Eight gilded lines radiate outwards from the rivet, dividing the object into four decorative quarters. Within each quarter is a heart-shaped cell containing red enamel in two quarters, and blue enamel in the other.

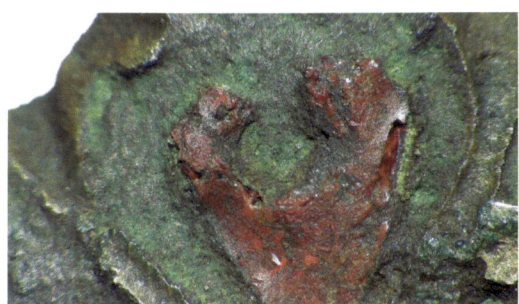 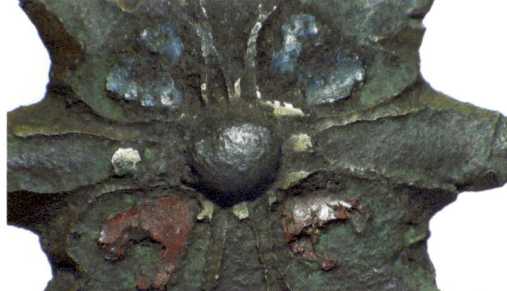

Left and right: Detail of the enamelling, viewed beneath a microscope.

Chapter 5
Post-Medieval (1540–1900)

Manchester began changing from a rural village to a busy market town during the sixteenth century, largely due to the growth of the wool trade. In the 1620s, the weaving of heavy cloth known as fustian and the arrival of Flemish weavers furthered the growth of the town. This focus on weaving based around the production of cotton eventually lead to Manchester becoming the first industrial city.

In and around the urban areas, small pockets of countryside remain, and it is here that single objects are found by metal detectorists, field walkers and gardeners. Finds of coins, medals and clothing fasteners remind us that, although much has changed, both trade and fashion remain as important to people today as they were to those who went before us. Alongside single objects lost by individuals, the archaeology of Greater Manchester remains clearly visible in today's landscape where post-medieval and early modern mills dating from the late eighteenth to early nineteenth centuries dot the horizon.

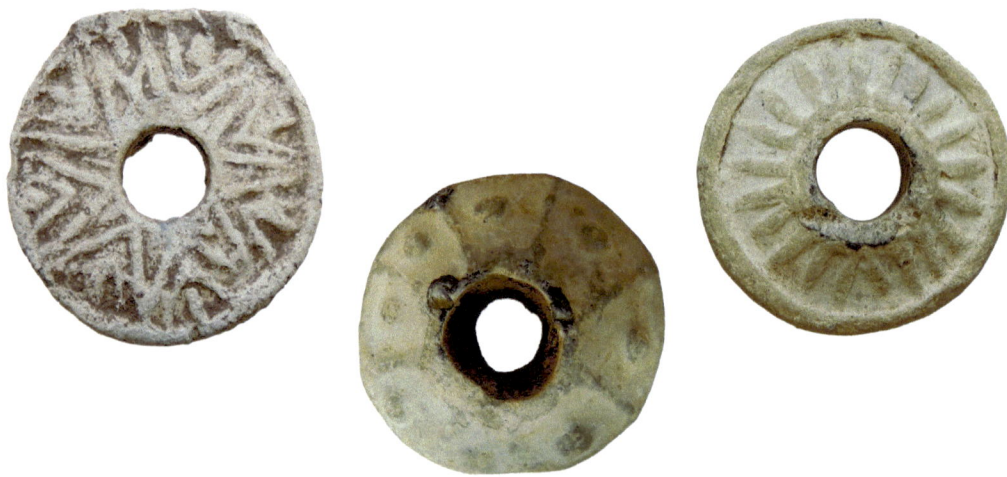

Spindle whorls were used for spinning wool into thread to weave or knit.

22. Silver-gilt dress fastener (LVPL-AD4E63/2004 T108)
Post-Medieval (AD 1500–1600)
Discovered in 2004 in Marple, acquired by Stockport Museums. Length 22.5 mm.

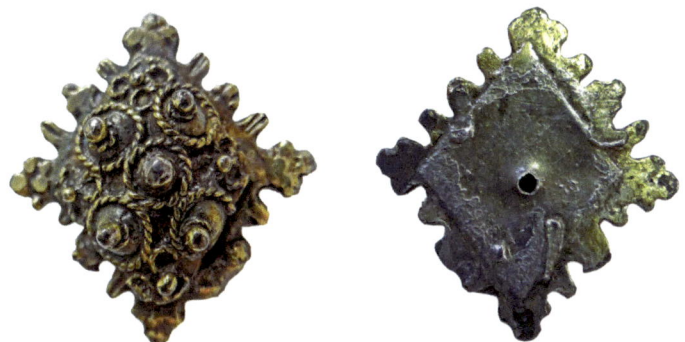

(Copyright Stockport Museums. Reproduced with kind permission)

Hooks and clasps were a popular way of fastening clothing during the sixteenth and seventeenth centuries. They are both practical and fashionable; many, such as this example, were cast in silver and then gilded. The fastener is composite, having a lozenge-shaped back plate with a fleur-de-lis at each apex and hand-cut serrated edges. On top of the plate sits a hollow cast cushion, decorated with five rounded knops, each encircled with filigree wire. The hook that would have connected with a similarly decorated plate with an 'eye' fastener is missing.

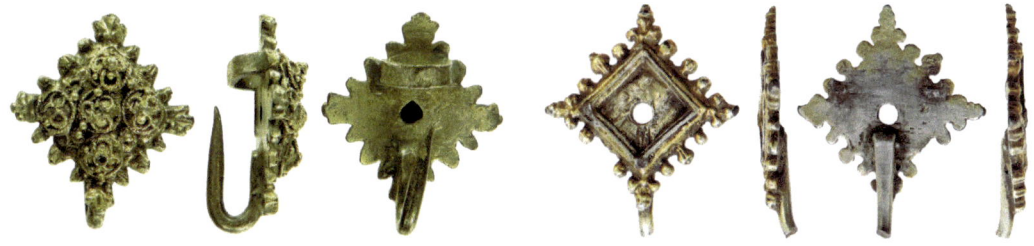

Left: LVPL-16EEF8: a complete example from Nantwich with similar decoration – acquired by Nantwich museum.

Right: LVPL-B16A24, discovered in Cheshire, is similar but it has lost its hollow cast cushion, revealing the back plate.

23. Silver groat of Henry VIII (LVPL-A4DE66)
Post-Medieval (AD 1532–1542)
Discovered in 2014 in Heald Green. Diameter 25.05 mm.

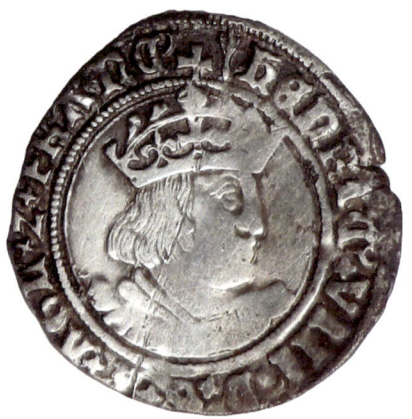 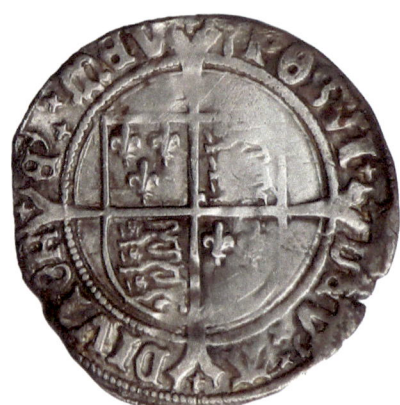

This silver groat shows the crowned portrait of Henry VIII facing right, surrounded by the legend *'HENRIC VIII D G R AGL Z FRANC'*. This translates as *'Henry VIII by the Grace of God King of England and France'*. The rear of the coin depicts a long cross fourchée over the royal shield and reads *'POSVI DEV' ADIVTORE' MEV'*. This translates as *'I have made God my helper'*. One of the most well-remembered monarchs, as much as for his personal as well as his political life, the coins of Henry VIII show an unfamiliar but distinctive portrait with a large blunt nose – not just a generic depiction, as occurs on many earlier coins.

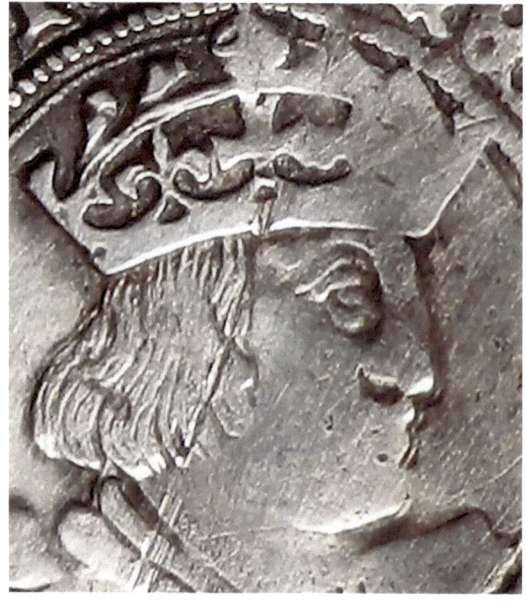

24. Gold unite of Charles I (LVPL-26EC55)
Post-Medieval (AD 1626–1627)
Discovered in 2015 in Barton. Diameter 34 mm.

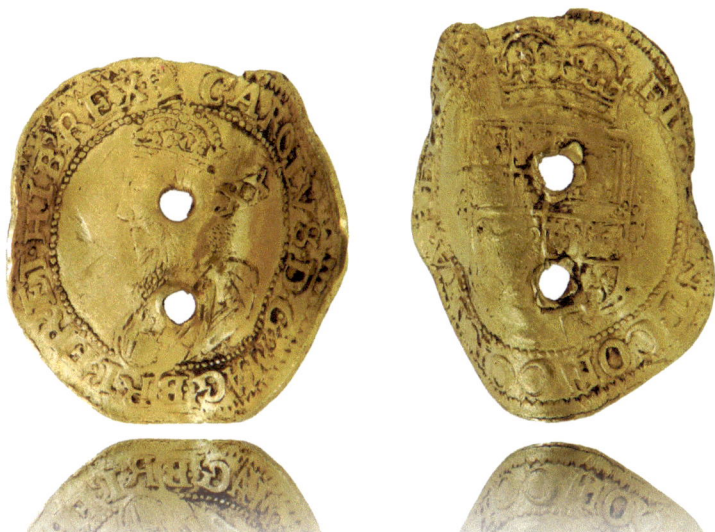

This gold unite originally had the face value of £1, which equates today to a face value of almost £100. The coin depicts the crowned bust of Charles I facing left, with XX stamped behind the bust. The legend around the edge reads '*CAROLVS D G MAG BRI FR ET HIB REX*', which translates as 'Charles, by the Grace of God King of Great Britain, France and Ireland'. The reverse of the coin shows the royal crowned shield and reads '*FLORENT CONCORDIA REGNA*', 'Kingdoms flourish through concord'. The initial mark at the start of the legend is known as a Moor's head; initial marks were changed periodically and this is how we know the coin was made between 1626 and 1627. The coin has been deliberately pierced in two places with very large holes that appear to be aligned across the shield; both holes were punched from the front to the back and the spall was hammered flat.

The piercing of the coin and subsequent loss of weight could suggest this coin was removed from circulation as currency and used for another purpose. An alternative theory could be that the holes were cut to deface the King's portrait. There is, however, no evidence that this was a widespread practice and reducing the value of a gold coin is unusual.

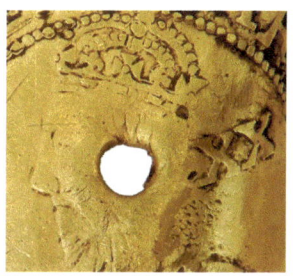

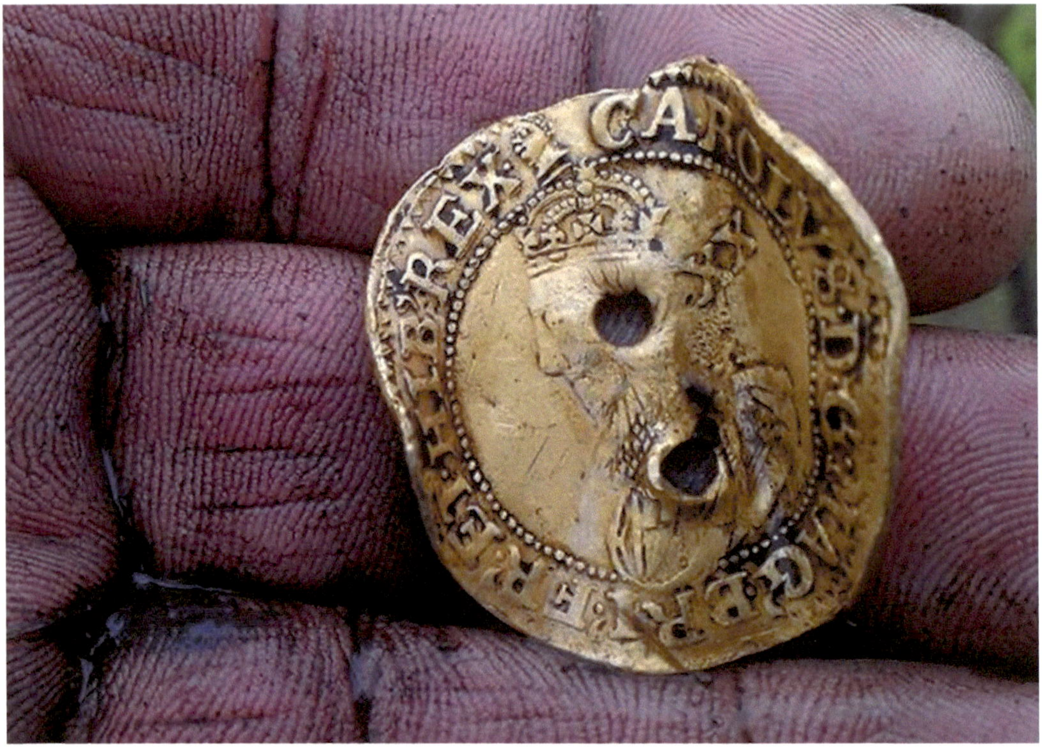

The coin immediately after discovery.

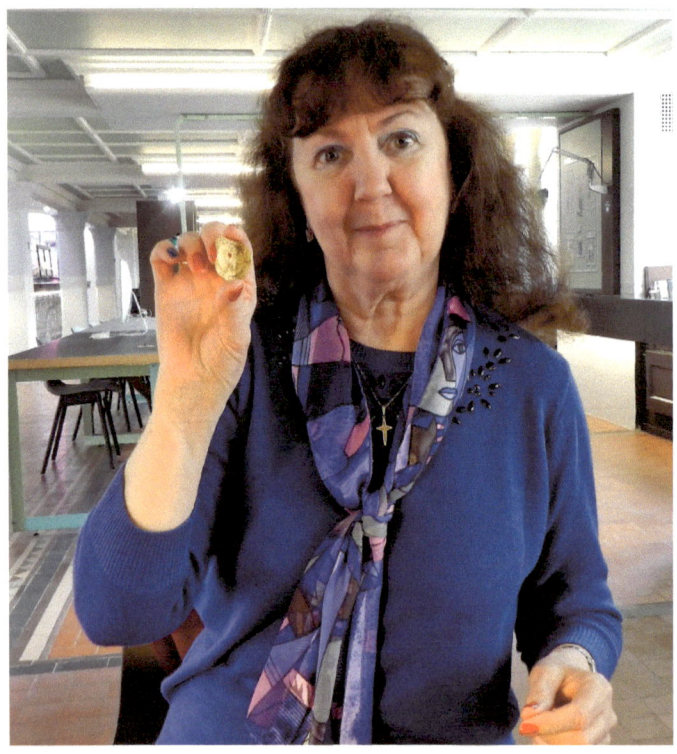

Detectorist Kath Read collecting her coin at Manchester Museum following its submission as a potential Treasure case.

25. Copper-alloy medal (LANCUM-E564F0)
Post-Medieval (AD 1500–1700)
Discovered in 2010 in Littleborough. Diameter 43.84 mm.

This medal celebrating marriage may be post-medieval in date but it could also be a later British copy of an earlier German marriage medal. The inscription reads '*VNANIMI VIGEANT CORPORA JVNCTA FIDE*'. This translates as 'living in harmony, joined into one body by faith'. The front face of the medal shows a single standing body with two heads – a male (right) and female (left). Flanking the body on either side are cupids or *putti*; the one on the right holds a banner, while the one on the left grasps a horse shoe as a sign for good luck/fortune. The reverse face has a floral interlocking design. It is possible that this medal was made by Paul Walther, a well-known maker of medals in Dresden (modern Germany). Many of these commemorate weddings and anniversaries, and were made as presents on both public and private festive occasions.

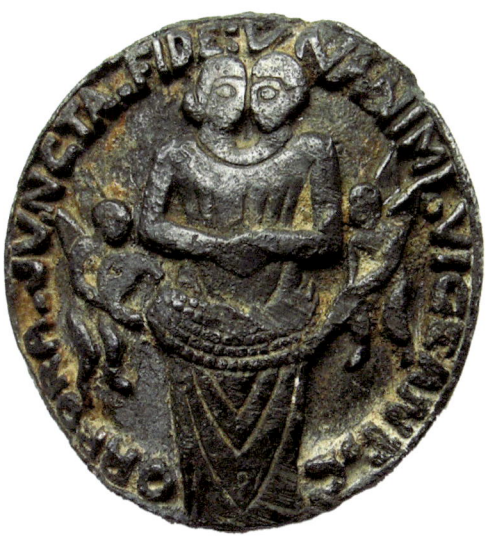
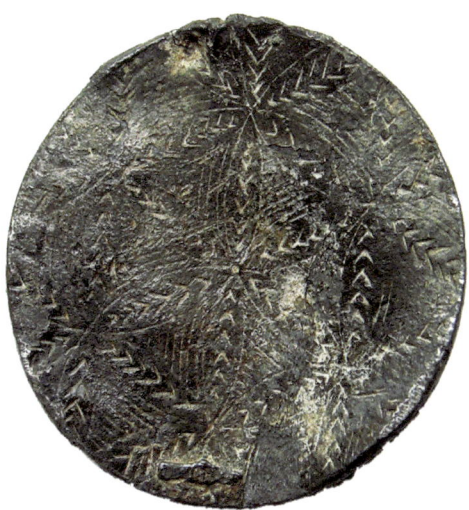

Part Two
Merseyside

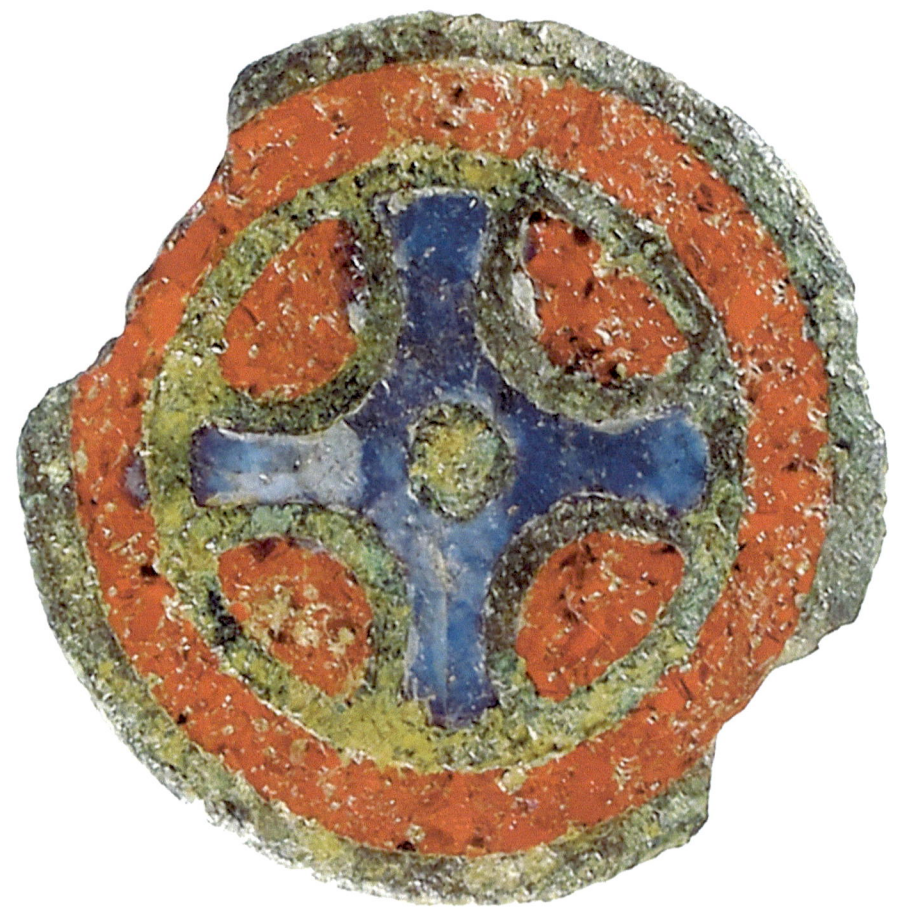

An example of the kind of decoration you may find on a Roman disc brooch, such as the one discovered in 2014 in Sefton.

Chapter 6
Prehistory (500,000 BC–AD 42)

Merseyside has several significant archaeological sites; some have been recently discovered, while others were investigated by the early antiquarians in the nineteenth century. Recently a nationally important site has been discovered in Lunt Meadows, Sefton. Excavations, led by Museum of Liverpool archaeologist Ron Cowell, have revealed some of the first houses in Britain dating back to 5,800 BC (similar to the famous Star Carr in Yorkshire).

The footprints of prehistoric people in Merseyside have been left behind in clay at Formby beach. These were formed between 5,400 and 2,300 BC by several family groups. Adult, children, auroch and red deer prints have been recorded, providing a glimpse into prehistoric life in the North West. On the opposite side of Liverpool (Childwall) we find the

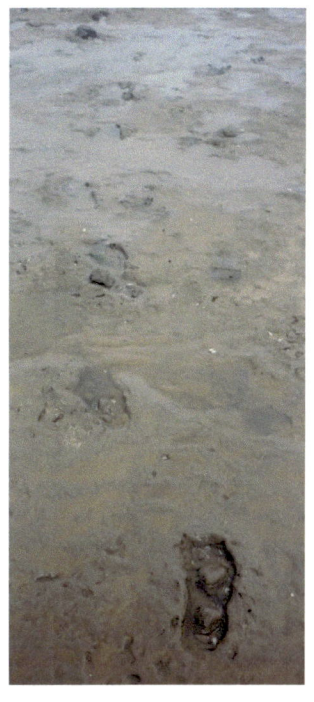

Prehistoric footprints at Formby. (Sam Rowe)

impressive Calderstones, which may have once formed part of a chambered tomb. Later prehistory is evident from Iron Age farms excavated at Irby, Halewood and Lathom.

Evidence of the people who lived simple lives in rural communities can be found in the archaeological record. More often their story is revealed through recorded chance finds discovered by metal detector users, field walkers, gardeners and farmers. These are the objects that are recorded on the PAS database and, by carefully plotting where they are found, we can discover a snapshot of past lives. Of the following finds, some are significant due to their rarity or what they can tell us, while others are more common finds. These everyday objects, when clear grid references are recorded, can provide us with valuable information about our past that would otherwise be lost.

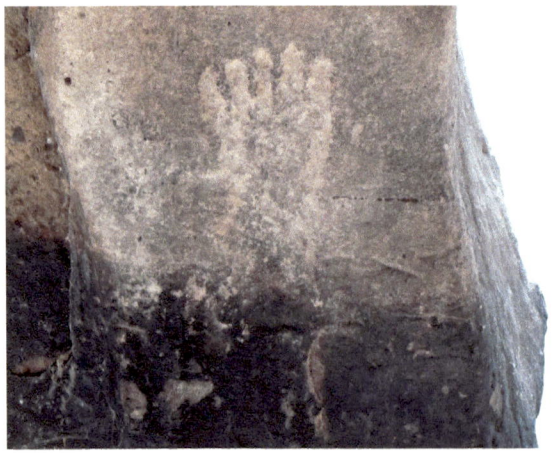

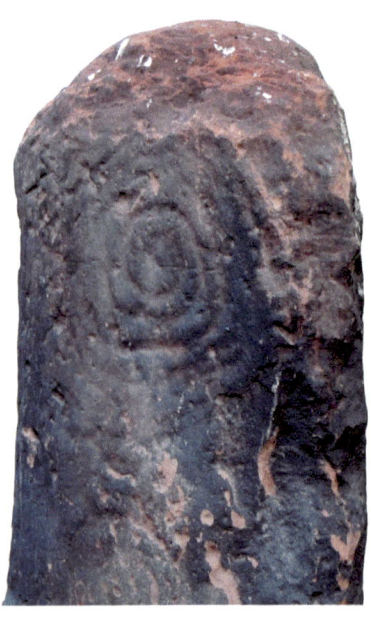

The Calderstones. (Trustees of National Museums Liverpool)

Neolithic (4000–2351 BC)

26. Stone axe head (LVPL-882DAE) MOL.1969.219.
Neolithic (3500-2100 BC)
Discovered in 1969 in Bidston, acquired by Museum of Liverpool. Length 130 mm.

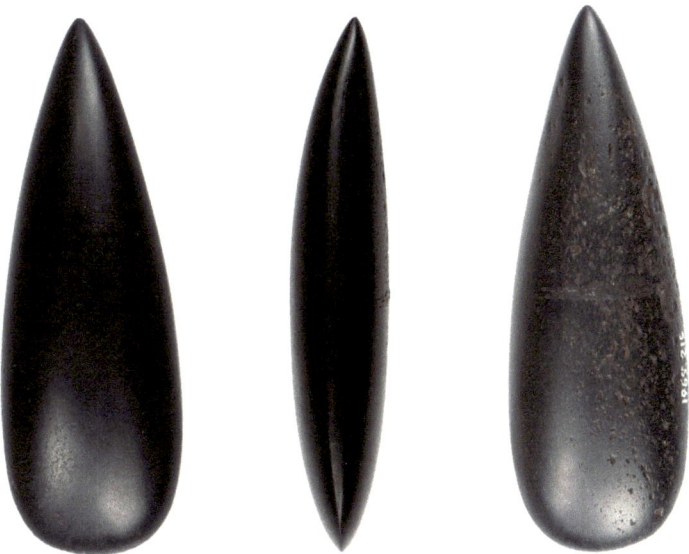

This beautiful stone axe has been ground and polished smooth. The axe is a pointed oval in cross-section with a wide cutting edge and is a mottled dark brown-black in colour. Axes such as these were essential tools for the Neolithic peoples, allowing them to clear woodland and build houses. They were hafted using a wooden handle and leather or string-like bindings.

This axe may have been sourced from County Antrim where a Neolithic quarry sits at the foot of Tievebulliagh Mountain. Axes from Tievebulliagh or Rathlin Island off the Antrim Coast, where this rare rock type also occurs, have been found across Britain. Similar teardrop-shaped axes of Tievebulliagh porcellanite can be seen in the Malone Hoard, which contains nineteen polished stone axes.

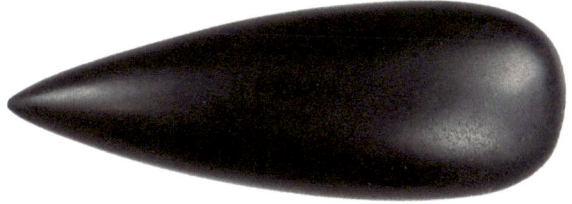

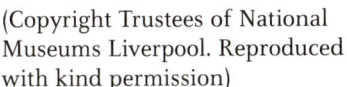

(Copyright Trustees of National Museums Liverpool. Reproduced with kind permission)

27. Stone axe head (LVPL-FA1F01)
Neolithic (4000–2500 BC)
Discovered in 1984 in Caldy. Length 79.38 mm.

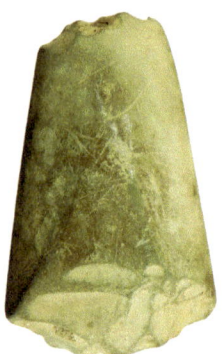 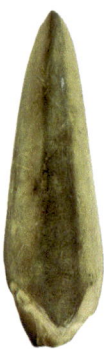 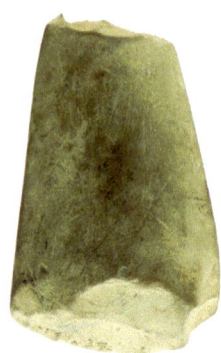

The butt of this polished stone axe head has been rubbed smooth. It has been broken either by movement in the plough soil or through use in antiquity. The faces and edges of the axe are worn with scratch marks, and the polished surface is faded. The stone is a light greenish brown colour and may be a volcanic tuff (compressed volcanic ash) rock originating from the Langdale Pike area of the Lake District. Langdale axes are one of the most common types of stone axe discovered in Britain.

Axes were not just practical tools; it is thought they had a symbolic function too. Volcanic tuff has a dense but well-structured matrix, allowing it to be shaped and flaked as flint is. When the axe has been roughed out, it is then polished. This polishing takes many days before a smooth burnished surface is achieved. To invest so much time in such a task suggests that the community invested value and possibly other symbolism into this humble tool.

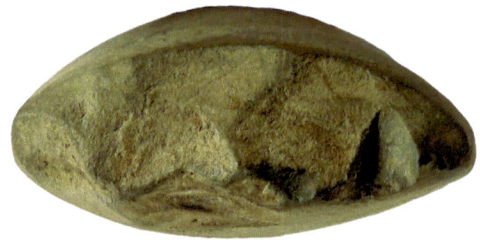

The butt end.

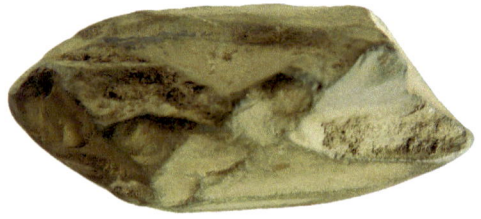

The cutting edge.

Bronze Age (2350–801 BC)

28. Flint arrowhead (LVPL-1A2E13)
Early Bronze Age (3000–2100 BC)
Discovered in 2006 in Greasby. Length 34 mm.

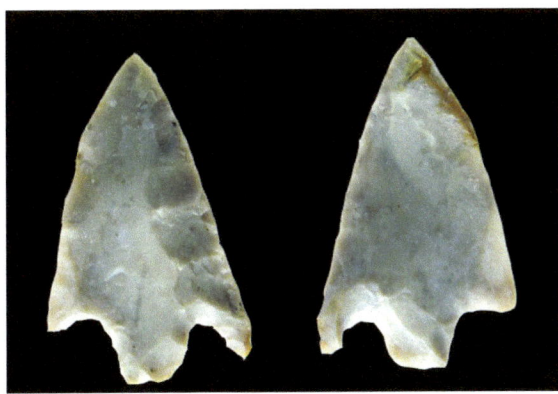

This barbed and tanged arrowhead has been carefully shaped to form a tool both of practical use and beauty. Made from a light, grey-coloured flint, it is remarkably small; one of the barbs has broken off, possibly during use. Unusually, a very small fragment of the brown cortex, the original outer skin on a flint nodule or pebble, remains at one end. This is usually removed when a piece of flint is worked into a tool. The long edges of the blade have been retouched with fine pressure flaking; this is most evident on the side where the barb is still present. Barbed and tanged arrowheads are a product of the very end of the Neolithic and Early Bronze Age. They were used for hunting, but were also buried with the dead in graves under round barrows.

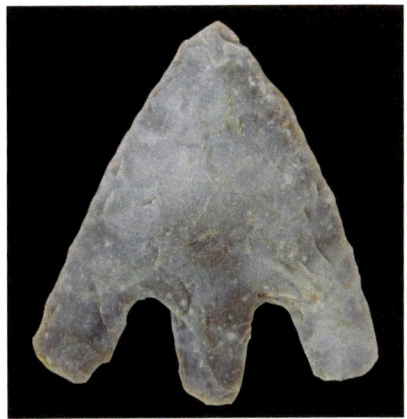

LVPL-88B913: A similar arrowhead found in Middlewich, Cheshire.

29. Copper-alloy developed flat axe head (LVPL-37DCA6)
Middle Bronze Age (1850–1750 BC)
Discovered in 2012 in Rainford. Length 103.5 mm.

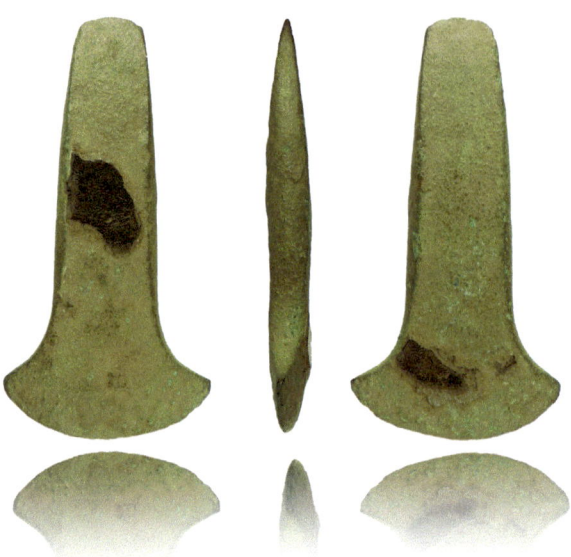

This is a narrow-butted developed flat axe dating from the very end of the Early Bronze Age of the beginning of the Middle Bronze Age. It is developed from the flat-axe form as it has a cast proto stop ridge, and raised flanges on the middle part of the body. The axe also has straight sides, a rounded butt and a flared cutting edge with concave shoulders. The stop ridge prevented the axe from being driven into the handle during use, and the raised flanges stopped lateral movement / wobble. The tips of the crescent-shaped blade have been damaged through abrasion or wear, as has the blade edge itself. The majority of the patina has broken away, leaving just two small patches on each face. One patch of smooth, dark-brown patina shows up the proto stop ridge. The development of the stop ridge occurred in part due to changing hafting methods. A knee handle with a forked angled end was preferred, resulting in the axes becoming narrower in order to fit snugly.

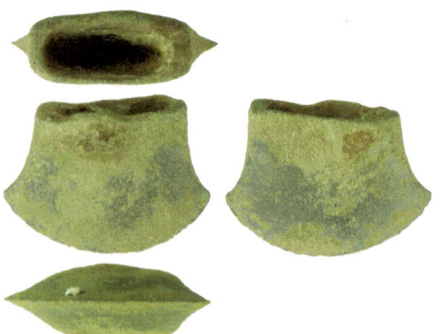

LVPL-906253, a fragment of a late Bronze Age socketed axe (1000–800 BC) discovered close by in Rainford.

30. Copper-alloy socketed spearhead (LVPL-68BF43)
Middle Bronze Age (1500–1200 BC)
Discovered in 2013 in Knowlsey. Length 78.35 mm.

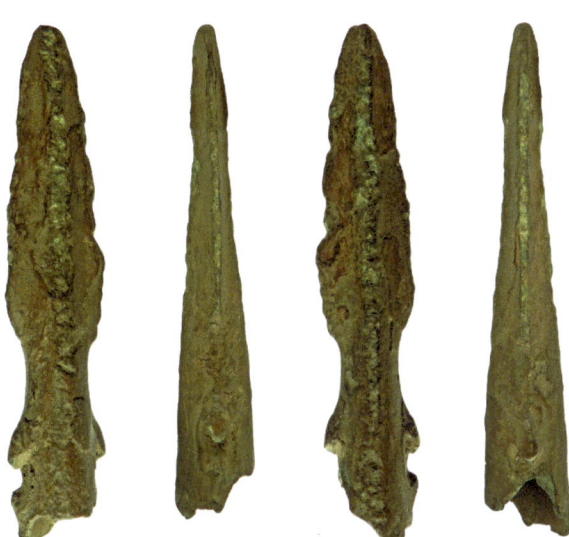

This socketed, side-looped spearhead is almost complete. The head is leaf-shaped and the socket has a pronounced midrib. The midrib is lozenge shaped and extends to the base of the socket where it is slightly faceted rather than raised. The tip of the spearhead is missing. The edges of the blade have been damaged in most places and the cutting edges are lost. The string loops, which would have allowed the spearhead to be tied to the haft, are incomplete and the mouth of the socket is broken.

The Middle Bronze Age sees dramatic changes in casting technology, which enabled many more complex artefacts to be made. It also sees huge changes in the population, possibly in conjunction with a period of climate change that puts more pressure on farming and resources. It is at this time that we start to see overt weapons, such as spearheads like this, as well as swords and daggers being made. The militarisation of the population also extends to more defended community sites and sees a new monument type – the hillfort!

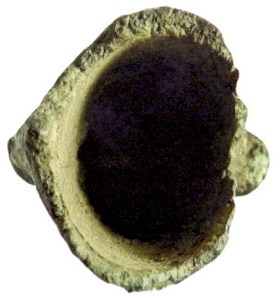

The socket.

Chapter 7
Roman (AD 43–409)

Fewer than 200 Roman objects have currently been recorded on the PAS database from Merseyside, with the majority clustering around the Wirral and Sefton. Most of the finds are coins or brooches – small objects that are easily lost. One of the most notable objects on the database, which takes its name from the area, is the Wirral brooch. A distinctive form of Roman brooch decorated with cells of brightly coloured enamel, the Wirral brooch, as noted by Philpott, is predominantly found in the North West. Only by plotting the grid references of finds can significant trends like this be discovered.

Prior to the existence of PAS, hundreds more Roman finds were discovered at the beach market at Meols on the North Wirral peninsula. These include numerous coins, brooches, earrings, grooming equipment, vessels, spindle whorls, pottery, building material and more. It was here that erosion of the sand at Dove Point during the nineteenth century revealed settlement sites and a wealth of archaeological finds. These objects from prehistory through to the post-medieval period were collected and documented by a group of Victorian antiquarians, most notably the Reverend Abraham Hulme. An Irishman from Co. Down, with a degree from Trinity College Dublin, Hulme published many of the objects in his 1863 book *Ancient Meols*. Many of these finds are now housed in the Museum of Liverpool and Grosvenor Museum, Chester. More recently the discoveries have been brought together in the publication by Griffiths, Philpott and Egan in *Meols – The Archaeology of the North Wirral Coast* (2007). The landscape of this coastline has changed considerably since ancient times, a fact highlighted by the remains of the 'Ancient Forest'.

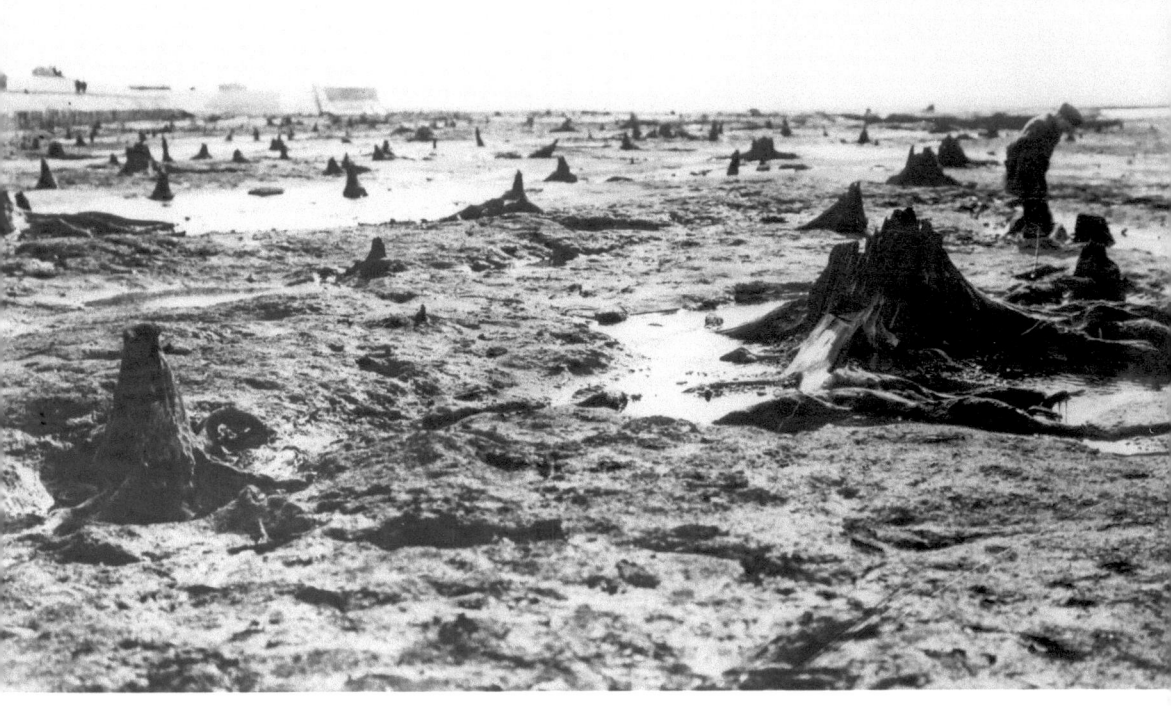

The 'Ancient Forest' at Meols, photographed in 1913. (Trustees of National Museums Liverpool)

31. Copper-alloy *nummus* (LVPL-F09323)
Roman (AD 335–331)
Discovered in 2009 in Liverpool. Diameter 16 mm.

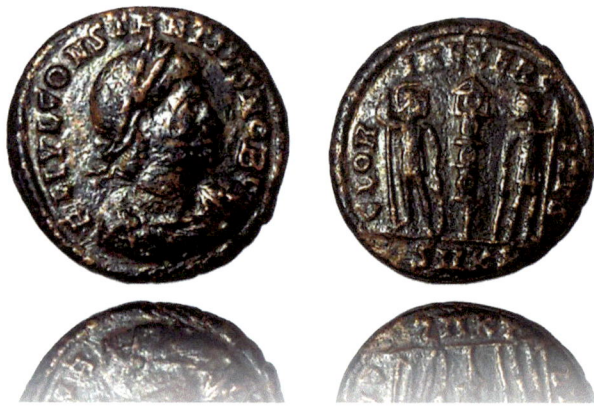

This *nummus* of Constantius II (AD 337–361) depicts the emperor facing right with a laureate crown. The obverse legend reads *'FL. IVL. CONSTANTIVS NOB.C'*, which translates as 'Flavius (Sons of Constantine) junior Constantius most noble Caesar'. The reverse of the coin depicts two soldiers with spears either side of a standard, and the inscription reads *'GLORIA EXERCITVS'*. This translates as *The Glory of the Army*. Beneath the soldiers are the letters *'SMK[A]'*; this tells us the coin was minted in Cyzicus in the Eastern Empire (in the south of modern-day Turkey). This coin was found by a passer-by on a spoil heap from modern construction in Liverpool city centre.

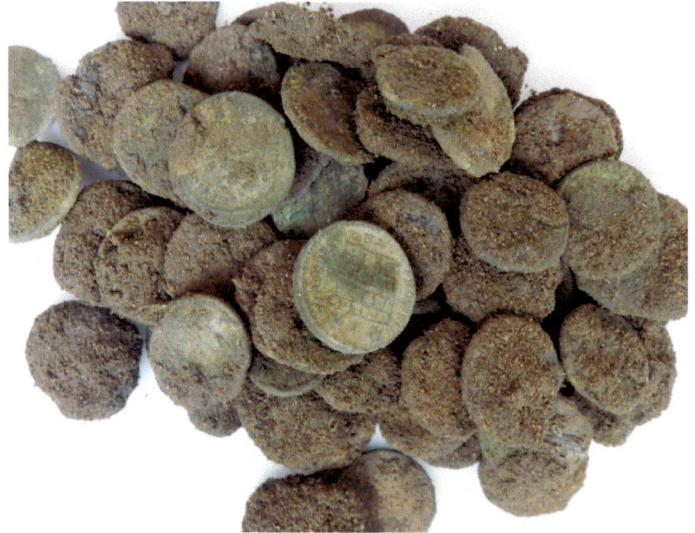

LVPL-8CC2AC: A hoard of similar coins, known as the Poole hoard, were discovered near Nantwich, Cheshire in 2016.

32. Copper-alloy disc brooch (LVPL-B54166)
Roman (AD 80–250)
Discovered in 2014 in Sefton. Length 38 mm.

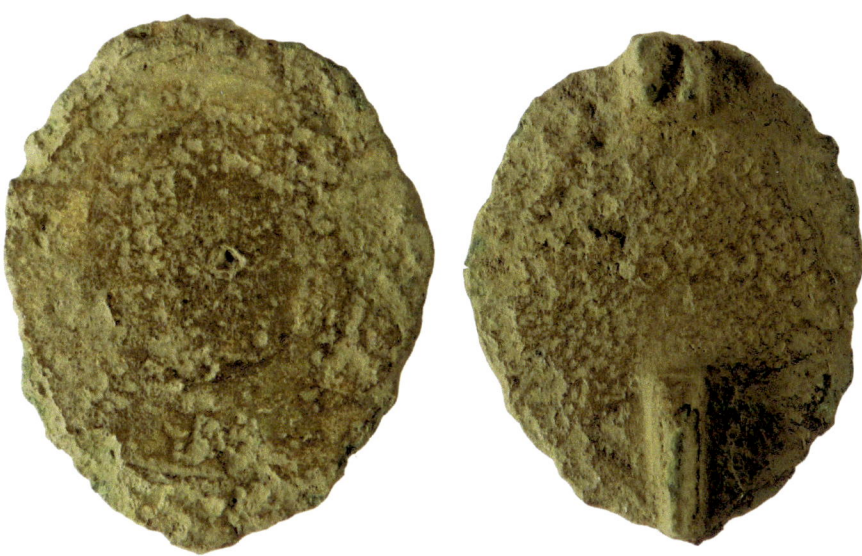

This Roman disc brooch is oval in plan, although all of the outer edges have been damaged by movement in the soil. The front is decorated with two slightly raised oval bands of copper alloy that surround a central circular depression. Originally the central element would have had a stone or possibly intaglio setting, while the oval border would have been inlayed with enamel. All this decoration is now lost. On the rear is a double lug, which would have housed the hinged pin, and a catch plate to secure the pin. Both the hinge and pin are missing. Each surface of the object is pitted and worn with a mid-brown patina.

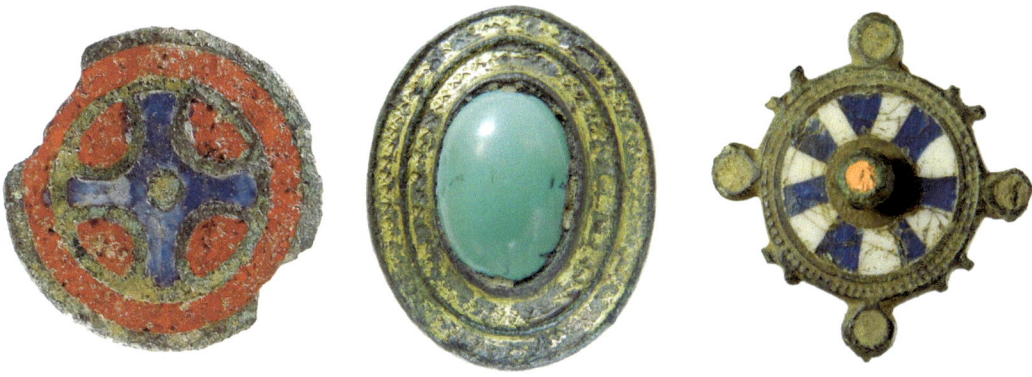

Some different types of decoration used on Roman disc brooches of similar date.

33. Copper-alloy Wirral brooch (LVPL-BFF3DB)
Roman (AD 100–200)
Discovered in 2014 in Thornton. Length 54.42 mm.

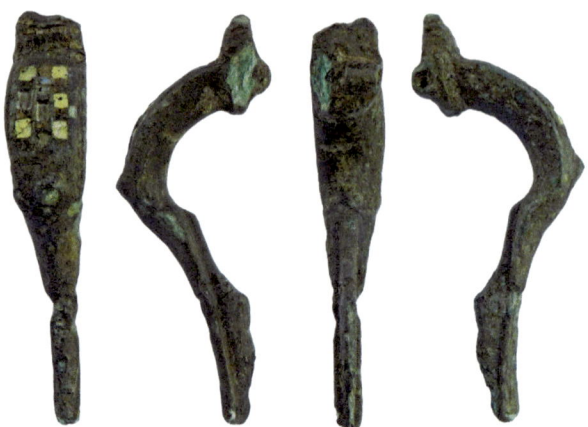

Wirral brooches, as the name suggests, were first noticed as being primarily found on the Wirral peninsula. Since their initial identification and classification by Philpott, their distribution has widened (following the work of former FLO for Cheshire, Greater Manchester and Merseyside Frances MacIntosh) but continues to be predominantly found in the North West of England and North Wales. These brooches derive from the trumpet brooch and date from the second century AD. The head of this brooch is stepped, which is typical of this type, and the head loop is missing due to ancient breaks. The upper bow is decorated with three raised vertical panels with alternating cells of yellow and blue enamel. Below the panels is a slight, raised rounded knop, which has been damaged. The bow tapers below the knop and terminates with an incomplete foot.

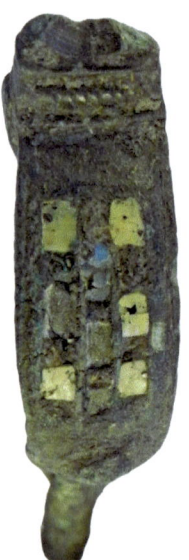

Left: Like modern football kits, the regional distribution of this brooch suggests the type may have identified the wearers as belonging to a particular group in society or having a certain belief.

Right: LVPL-036B5D: A more complete example from Wrexham; it retains the head loop but is missing the enamel.

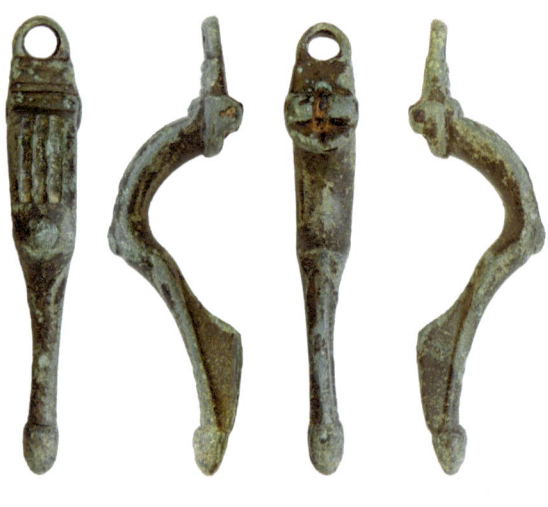

34. Ceramic vessel (LVPL-3B6BF5) MOL 1995.105.9999
Roman (AD 100–200)
Discovered in the 1940s in Irby, acquired by Museum of Liverpool. Diameter 165 mm.

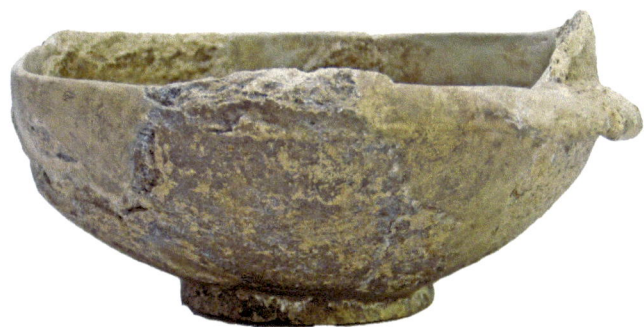

(Copyright Trustees of National Museums Liverpool. Reproduced with kind permission)

Roman pottery was produced in large industrial centres throughout Britain. This vessel is an imitation of a Samian flanged bowl, (classified as Dragondorf 38). Samian ware was first produced in Italy at the end of the first century BC, with most vessels being made in Gaul (France) by AD 43. This copy was made in England. The bowl is circular in plan, with a circular base, and is U-shaped in profile. The rounded rim is damaged in places. This vessel was discovered when previously uncultivated land was turned over to food production in the 'Dig for Victory' campaign during the Second World War. The finder Jim Rogers kept the bowl in his powdered milk tin for the next forty years before bringing it into National Museums Liverpool to show the curators. Jim's find and information lead archaeologists to undertake a large-scale excavation in 1992, resulting in the discovery of a new multi-period site, which provided evidence for a settlement at Irby from the Iron Age.

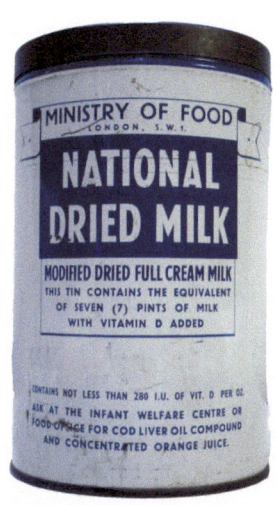

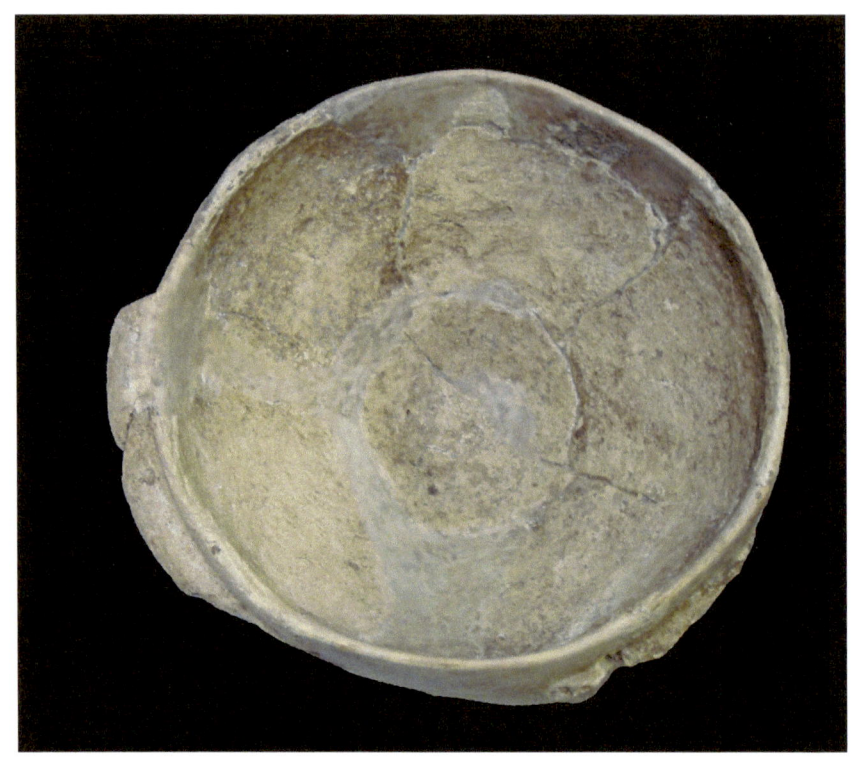
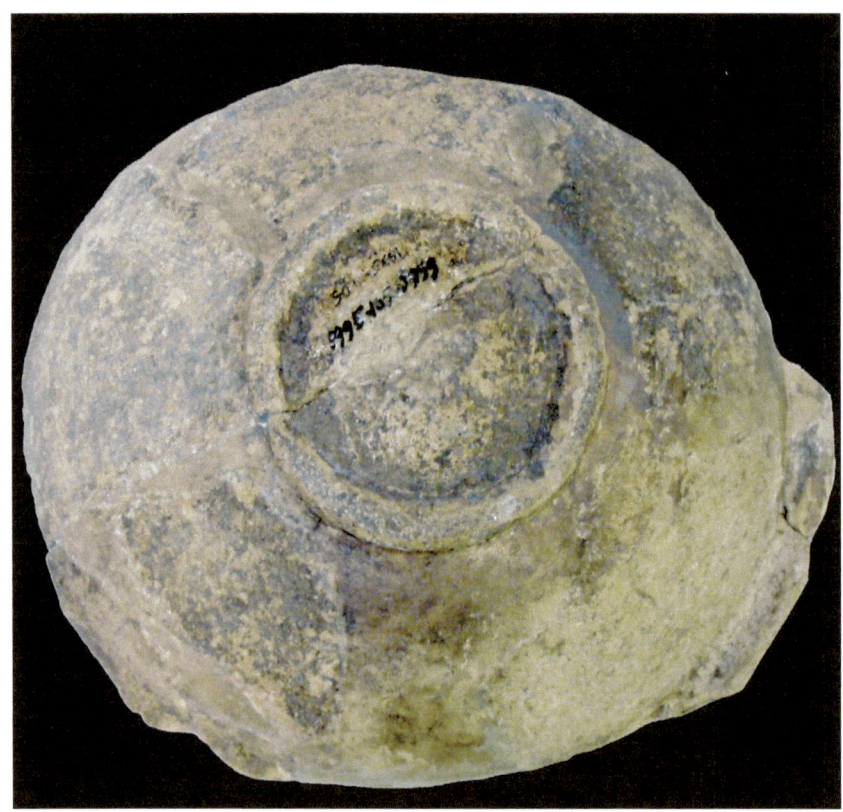

35. Copper alloy bracelet (LVPL-6A67D5)
Roman (AD 200–300)
Discovery date unknown found in Thurstaston. Diameter 85 mm.

This Roman bracelet or armlet is delicately decorated with a spiral clasp. The bracelet has a simple hoop with decorative spiral terminals. Each terminal of the object forms the opposite spiral twist, with two wires passing either side and wrapping around the bracelet behind each terminal. This type of bracelet dates to the fourth century AD. Similar examples were found in the Lankhills Cemetery, Winchester, where 444 inhumation and seven cremation graves were excavated by archaeologists.

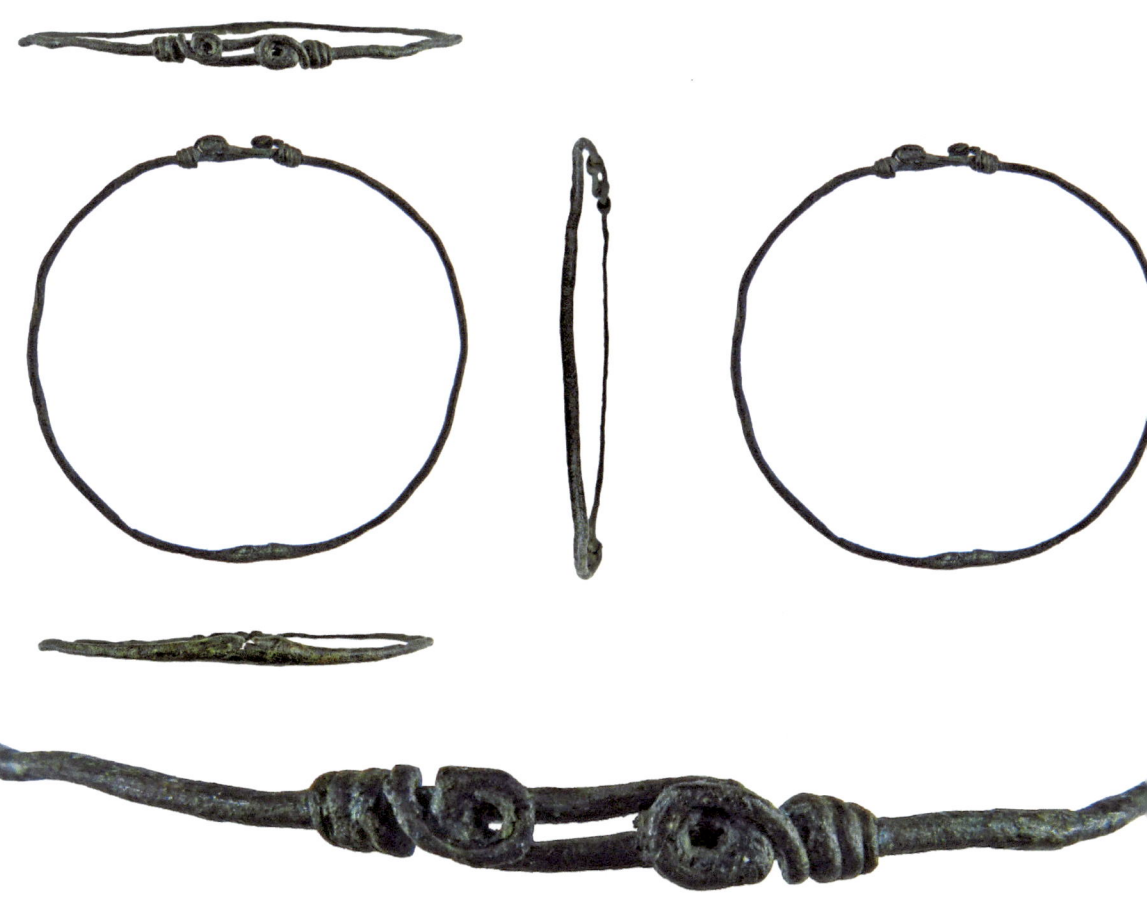

Chapter 8
Early Medieval (AD 410–1066)

The early medieval period in the North West is somewhat elusive. This is reflected in the number of objects and coins recorded on the PAS database, with just 282 records for the whole of the region. To the north and south of Merseyside, significant nationally important Viking hoards have been discovered. Frustratingly, to date there are only three early medieval finds recorded on the database – two of these were discovered in Sefton and are discussed below. The third find is a somewhat sad-looking stirrup strap mount from the Wirral, recorded as LVPL-557A12. Of course, while well-plotted chance finds can tell us much about what is happening in the landscape, their absence does not always mean that nothing occurred. The urbanised nature of Merseyside restricts the ability to discover objects by chance, while other factors such as permission from the landowner to metal detect and ease of access also come into play. An area devoid of finds does not always mean activity did not take place but rather that the evidence has not yet been found. Merseyside is part of the Irish Sea region, connected to Ireland and the Isle of Man by this important trade route, and should be seen as a landscape connected both by land and by sea. At West Kirby the tenth-century 'hogback' tombstone in St Bridget's Church also reminds us of the presence of the Vikings in Merseyside. Hopefully in years to come more finds will be recorded and we will be able to rewrite this chapter.

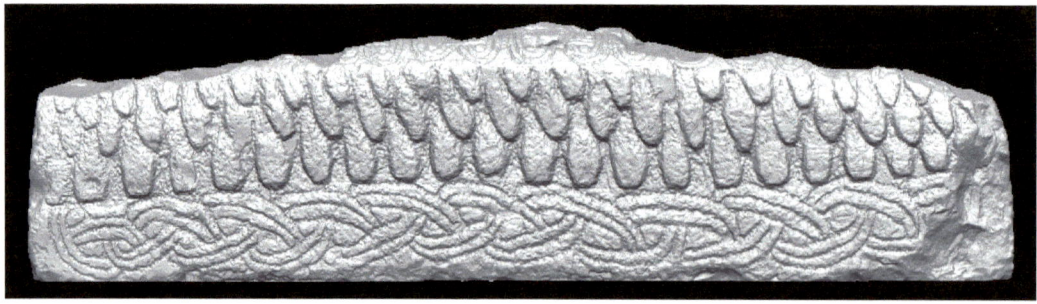

Laser scan image of the West Kirby 'hogback' tombstone. (Trustees of National Museums Liverpool)

36. Copper-alloy disc headed pin (LVPL-A6C291)
Early Medieval (AD 850–900)
Discovered in 2012 in Liverpool. Length 82.33 mm.

The pin has a flat, circular head, decorated with a pattern of five punched ring-and-dot motifs arranged around a central one. The back of the head is undecorated. The shaft is straight and tapers to a rounded point. The pin has a light-to-mid green rough patina and is corroded. Pins of this type date to the ninth century. The plate-headed types are most common after the Viking conquest of Yorkshire in AD 867, and this type of pin appears to have a northerly distribution, with examples known from the market site at Meols, the Viking grave at Knock-y-Doonee, Isle of Man, and also from Dublin, Whitby and York.

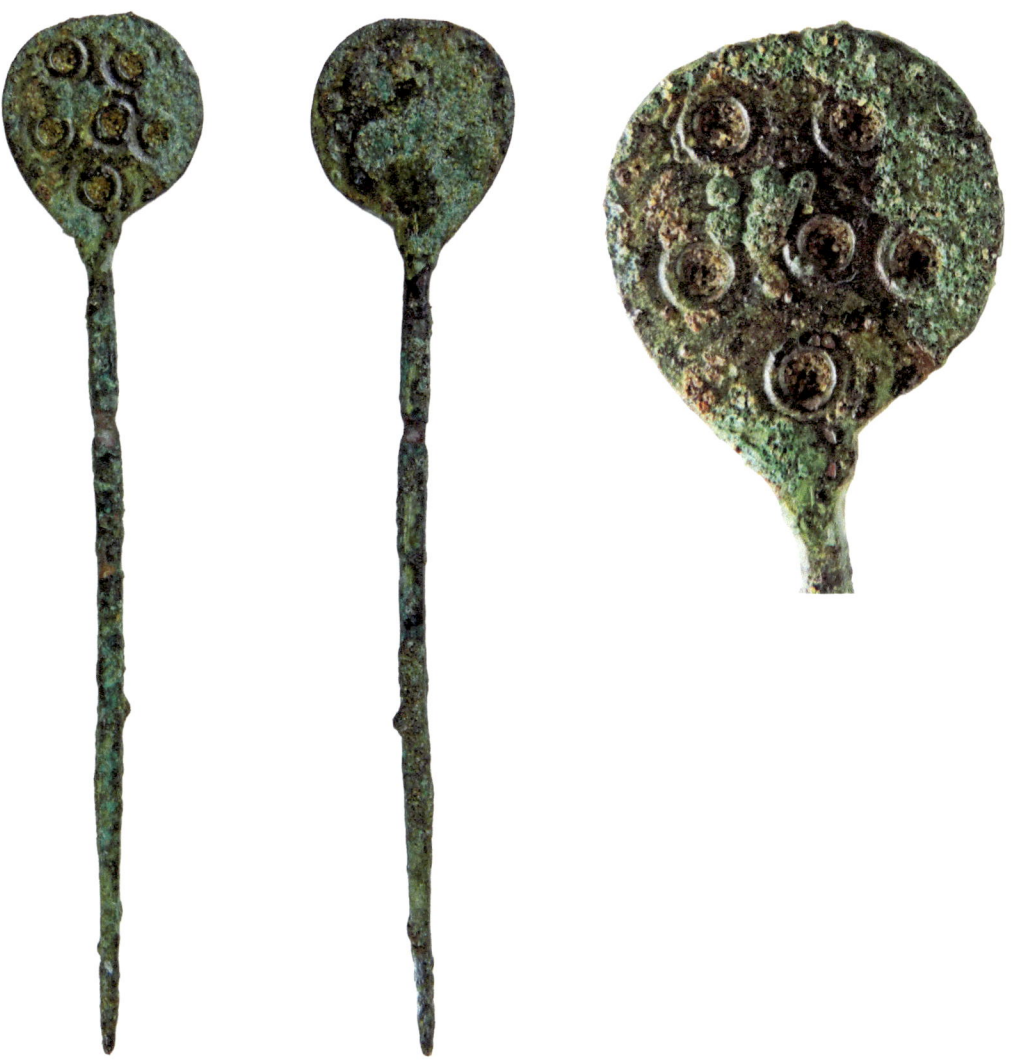

37. Copper-alloy strap end (LVPL-1E4442)
Anglo-Saxon (AD 800–900)
Discovered in 2010 in Formby. Length 26.62 mm.

Strap ends are used to strengthen the tip of a belt and stop the leather from fraying from use. This strap end has an attachment end, which is shaped around two circular rivet holes with a small projection in between. The front is decorated with a raised cross, each arm of which is decorated with a fine, longitudinal groove. The circular hole at the centre of the cross may have held a separate domed-headed rivet, which may have been silver. Nothing survives in the recesses between the cross-arms, although it may have had inlays of some kind. The four rectangular panels in the angles of the cross are keyed so that the solder used to apply the inlay would have something to grip. Traces of gilding can be seen on the arms of the cross and the attachment end. The lower part of the central panel, with the lower cross-arm, is missing as is the tip of the strap end. This would probably have had an animal-headed terminal.

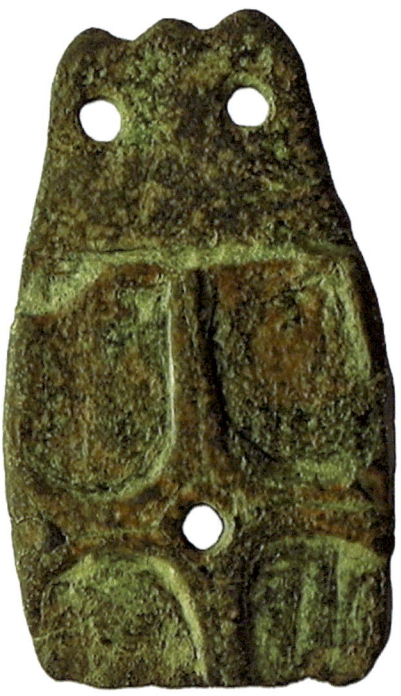 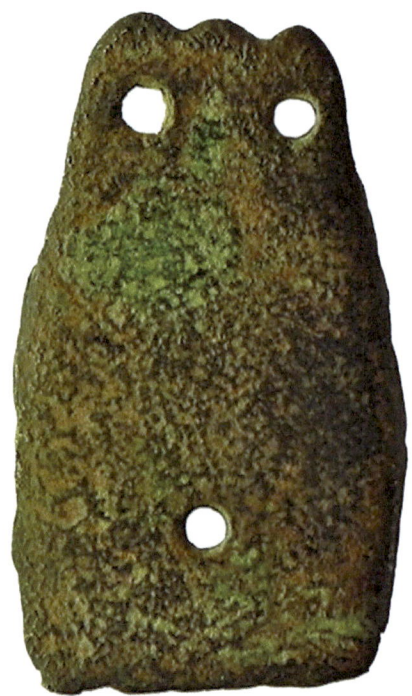

Chapter 9
Medieval (1066–1539)

The city of Liverpool began as a medieval port during the thirteenth century, receiving a royal charter from King John in 1207. The medieval finds recorded from Merseyside are typical of the period. Faith and religion were very important in medieval society and pilgrims' souvenirs were popular. The *ampulla* from Heswall, just one of over 1,500 recorded on the PAS database, was a popular type of souvenir, available to many with pennies to spare. Those with more money could purchase indulgences from the church – a reduction of time spent in purgatory in exchange for good deeds. It is likely that the Papal *bulla* from Whiston was attached to such a document.

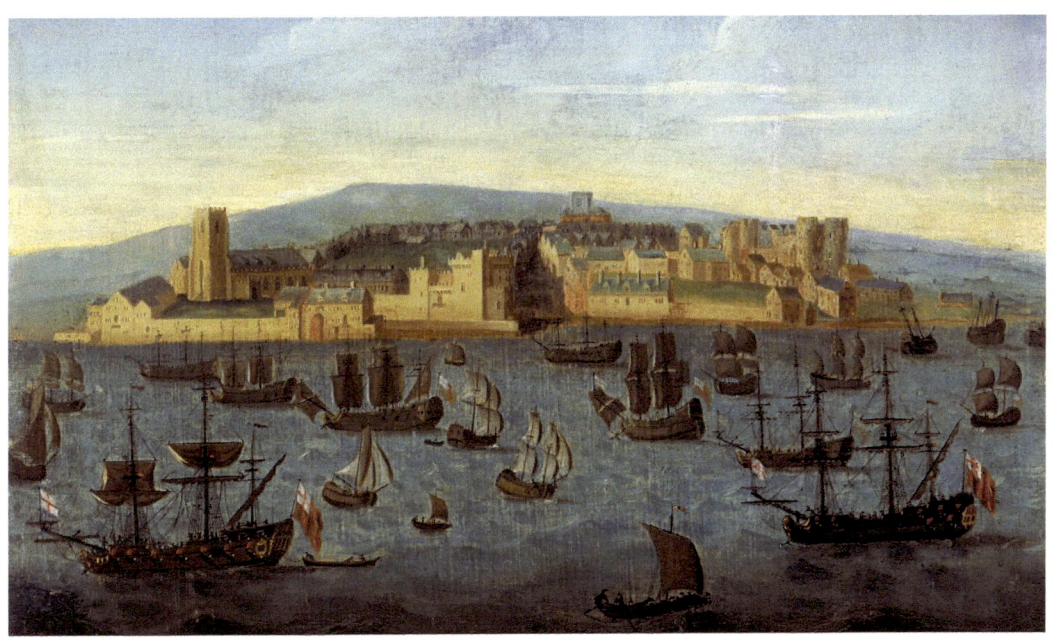

Peter's Portrait, the first known painting of Liverpool as a port in 1680. (Trustees of National Museums Liverpool)

38. Lead-alloy ampulla (LVPL-076916)
Medieval (AD 1350–1530)
Discovered in 2011 in Heswall. Length 50.09 mm.

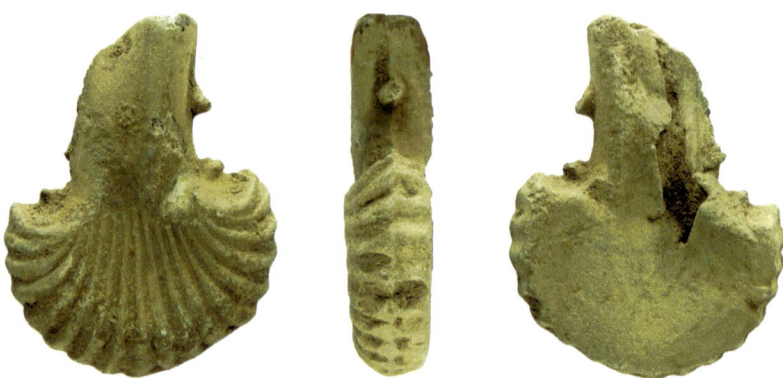

Ampullae (miniature phials) were often bought as pilgrims' souvenirs. They carried a dose / measure of the thaumaturgic (miracle-inducing) water given to pilgrims at many shrines and holy wells. The *ampulla* could have been worn as a talisman, suspended by two lugs on either side of the neck of the flask, or the water could have been taken to cure illness or disability. Other rural finds suggest that the water (and possibly the *ampulla* too) were part of the blessing of the fields rituals during the 'beating of the bounds'. This flask-like *ampulla* has a semi-circular bowl and long narrow neck, the top of which is open, having been split down one face. One surface of the *ampulla* is decorated with a scallop-shell design. The opposite face shows a large letter 'W' emblazoned on a shield within three concentric circles. *Ampullae* bearing a crowned W have been tentatively associated with the cult of Our Holy Lady of Walsingham.

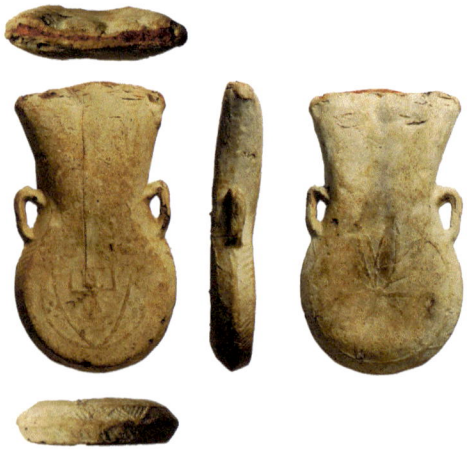

LVPL-DEA190: Ampulla with intact suspension luggs. This form dates to the last quarter of the twelfth century; *ampullae* were the only known pilgrim's souvenir used during the thirteenth century. In the early fourteenth century, their use was replaced by pilgrim's badges.

39. Silver penny (LVPL-B0645C)
Medieval (AD 1307–1309)
Discovered in 2015 in Melling. Diameter 16 mm.

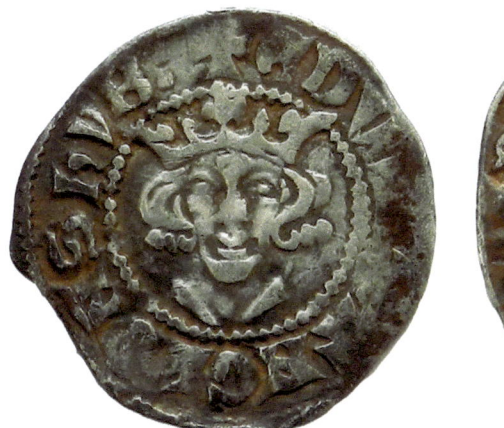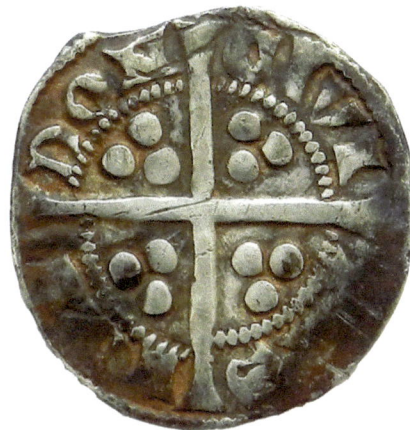

A 'sterling' penny of Edward I (AD 1272–1307) or Edward II (AD 1307–1327). The obverse of the coin depicts the King's crowned head facing forward and is surrounded with the legend '*EDWR ANGL DNS HYB*'. This translates as 'Edward King of England and Lord of Ireland'. On the reverse of the coin the legend reads '*CIVITAS LONDON*', informing us the coin was minted in London. The legend is interrupted by a long cross with three pellets in each quarter. This penny can be classified as class 10cf3, a group of coins produced between AD 1307 and 1309, the period marking the final days of Edward I and the start of Edward II's reign. The design and legends on these pennies remain unchanged for both rulers, and these coins are seen to define the standard for quality and fineness across Northern Europe – hence quality silver still being known as 'sterling'.

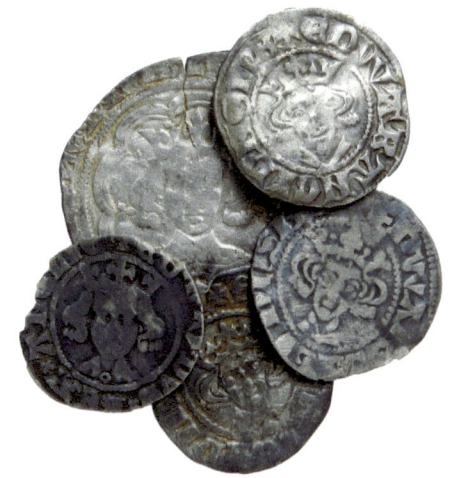

LVPL-5F033A: A small hoard from North Wales, including pennies of Edward I, II and III showing their similar busts.

40. Copper-alloy buckle plate (LANCUM-E07F03)
Medieval (AD 1300–1400)
Discovered in 2011 in Sefton. Length 45 mm.

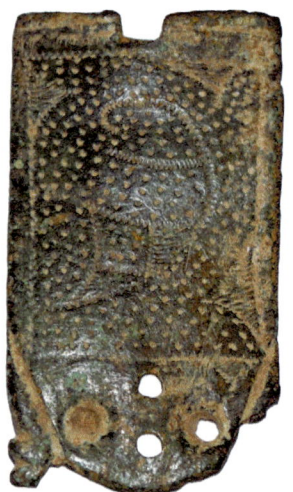 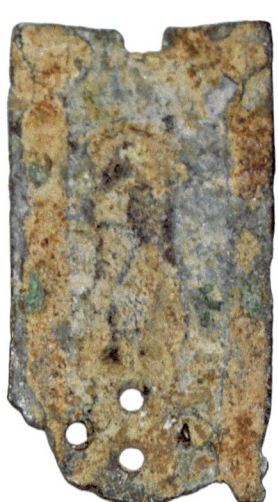

Buckles and buckle plates are very common finds, but this is an unusual example. The plate is formed from a cast sheet of copper alloy, which has been folded and cut to fit around the axis bar of a simple D-shaped buckle. The lower plate is pierced in four places, and it is likely that this is how it would have attached to a leather strap. The plate is decorated with massed punch marks delineating a man in a Phrygian cap (a soft conical cap that curls forward). This cap originated in Phrygia in modern Turkey, and was worn by freed slaves in the Roman period. The papal crown is based on the cap and this may be why it became popular in the medieval period, finally becoming the emblem of liberty during the eighteen-century French revolution. No exact dated parallels for this object have been found, although a fourteen-century date has been suggested.

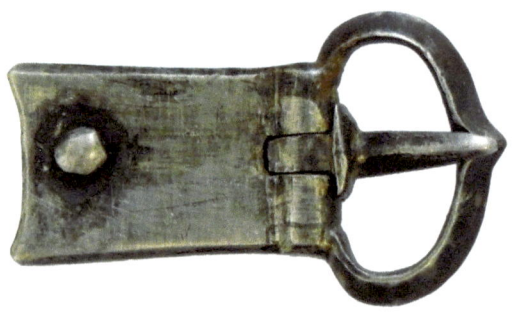 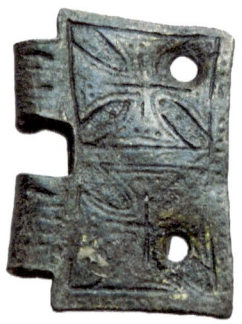

LVPL-0D70A8.   LVPL-F05DA2.

Left and Right: Different varieties of buckle plates used during the medieval period.

41. Lead-alloy papal bulla (PUBLIC-CE1262)
Medieval (AD 1389–1404)
Discovered before 2013 in Whiston. Diameter 37.96 mm.

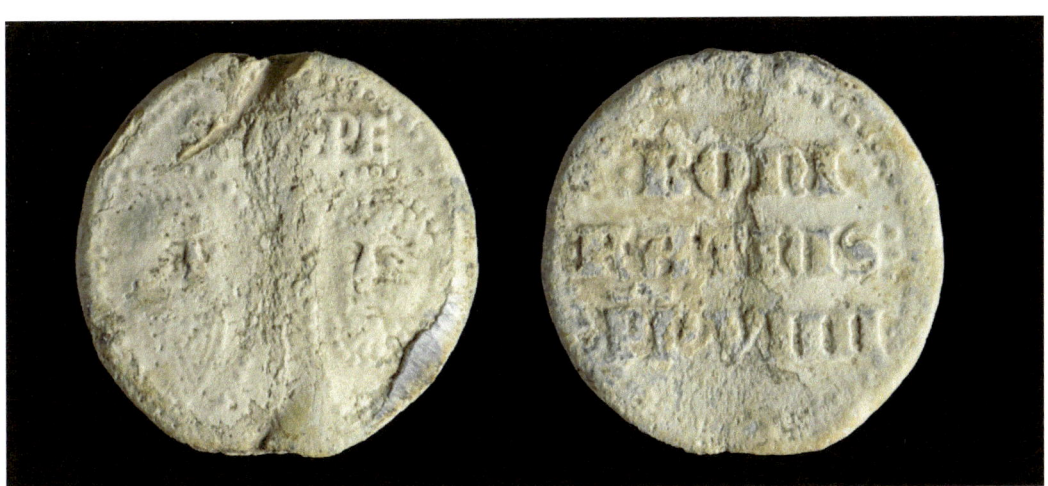

Papal *bulla* (lead seals) were fixed using waxen chords to official papal documents to authenticate their authority and provenance. This *bulla* is of Pope Boniface IX (AD 1389–1404). The front carries the name of the pope in three lines: '*BONI/FATIUS/PP VIIII*', translated as 'Boniface IX' with his abbreviated title (*Pastor Pastorum* – 'Shepherd of the Shepherds'). The opposite face shows the portraits of saints Paul and Peter beneath the letters 'SPA SPE' (an abbreviation standing for St Paul and St Peter). The first four letters are faint, and the portraits are worn. Between the two portraits there would have been a cross, but this has worn away. A cord would have entered and exited through the top and bottom of the object attaching it to the document.

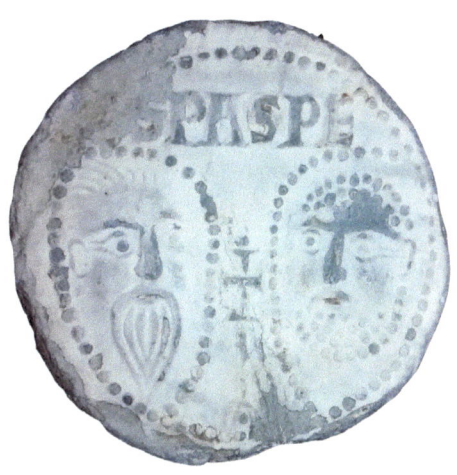

LVPL-0CEABB: St Paul and St Peter, depicted more clearly.

42. Gold half noble of Henry IV (1399–1413) (LVPL-004154)
Medieval (AD 1412–1413)
Discovered in 2012 in Bold. Diameter 25.12 mm.

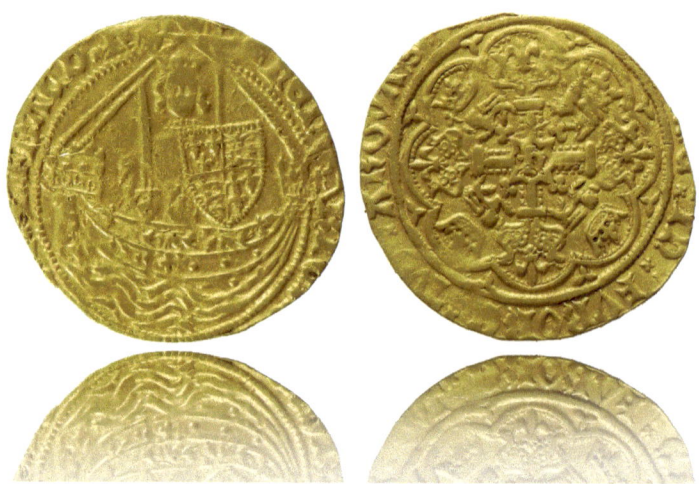

Gold nobles and half nobles are not commonly found as stray finds. This rare example of a gold coin is a half noble of Henry IV (1399–1413). The obverse (front) legend reads '*HENRIC DI GRA REX ANGL Z FRANC DNS HIB Z AQ*', which translates as 'Henry by the grace of God King of England and France, Lord of Ireland and Duke of Aquitaine'. The King stands in a ship, crowned, wearing armour and holding a sword and shield. The reverse reads, '*DOMINE NE IN FVRORE TVO ARGVAS ME*', taken from the Book of Psalms, Chapter 6, 'O Lord, rebuke me not in thine anger'. This penitential psalm is often depicted in medieval books of hours. The reverse is dominated by a floriated cross with a fleur-de-lis terminal at the end of each limb, contained within a tressure of eight arches. Within each angle of the cross is a lion with a crown above.

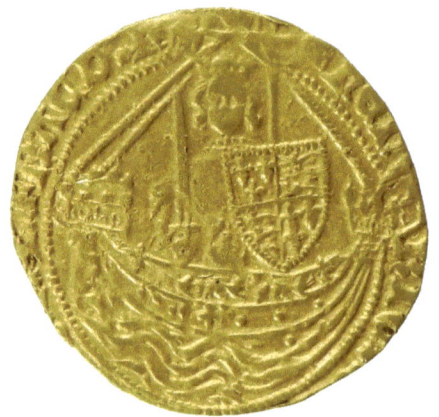

In the past twenty years, fewer than 400 gold medieval coins have been recorded on the PAS database out of over 1 million finds. This suggests that these coins would have been carefully guarded and looked after, being cashed in or melted down for their bullion value when they ceased to be legal tender.

43. Copper-alloy horse harness pendant (LVPL-D56392)
Medieval (AD 1400–1500)
Discovered in 2012 in Rainford. Length 49.25 mm.

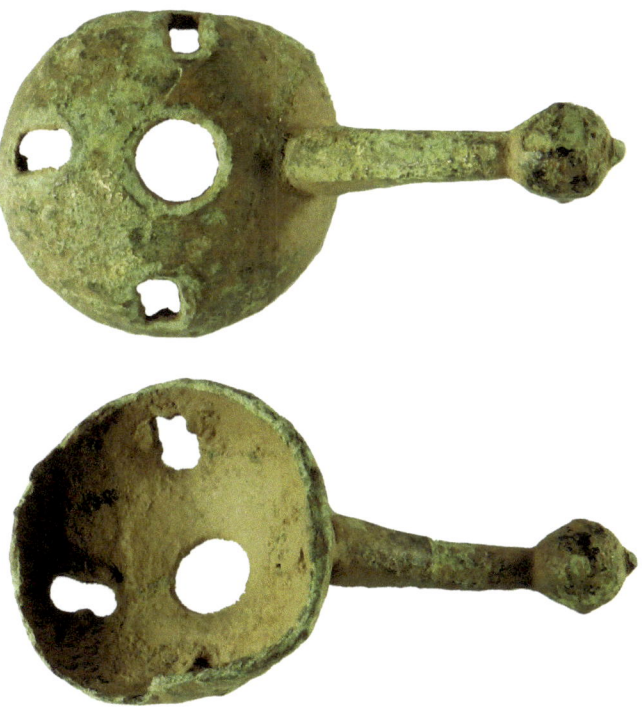

Harness pendants were popular in medieval England and would have identified the horse and rider as well giving an impression of the wealth and status of the rider. Corroded and dulled over time, this object would have been bright with gilding, as shown by remaining flecks. This harness pendant would have had two halves forming a sphere when complete. The rectangular holes would have each contained an 'arm' similar to the one remaining. The arm is held in place, flattening the end against the inside. This suggests that the arms were fixed into place before the missing upper half of the central sphere was fixed into place.

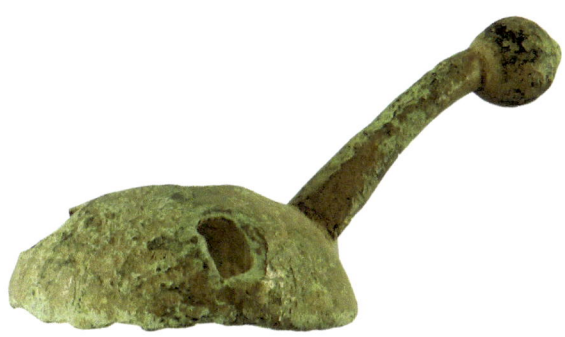

Chapter 10
Post-Medieval (1540–1900)

The post-medieval finds highlighted from Merseyside are typical, with small objects that were easy to get hold of and easy to lose. Some objects, however, have a stronger local connection than others. Following the opening of Liverpool old dock in 1715, the whole area gradually became more urban. The port of Liverpool remained small until a trading boom began in the eighteenth and nineteenth centuries. In the second half of the eighteenth century, Liverpool was a major slaving port with about fifty ships a year departing from

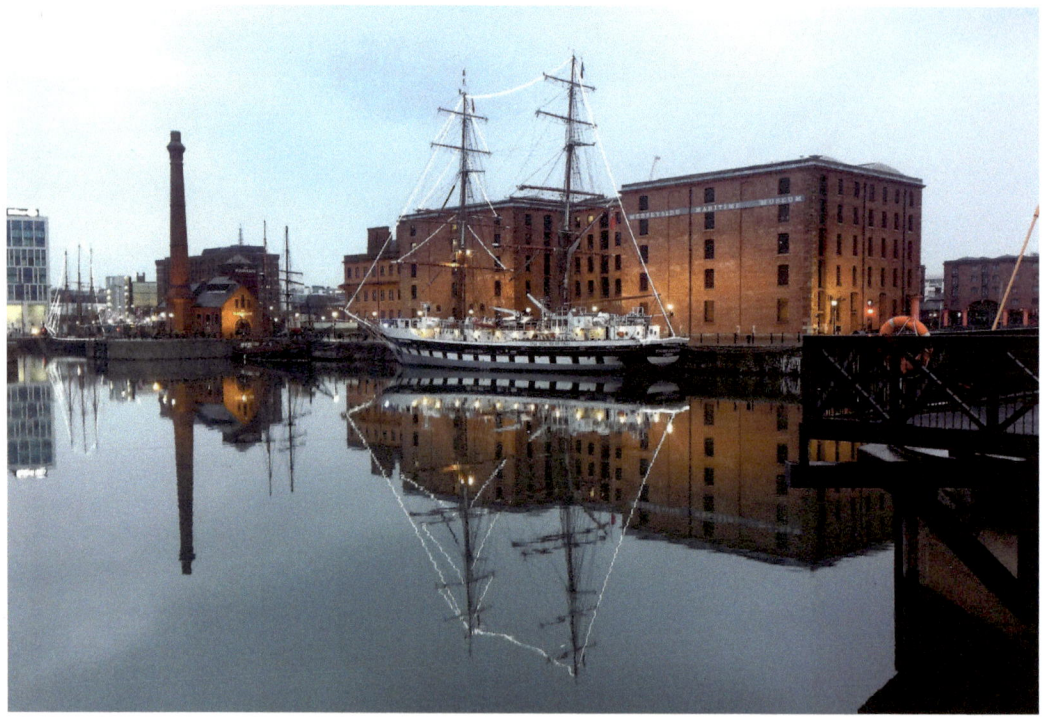

View across the docks to Merseyside Maritime Museum and the International Slavery Museum.

Liverpool in the 1750s. The brightly coloured trade beads below are a poignant reminder of the human cost to Liverpool's prosperity.

Occasionally, a chance find can lead to more extensive excavation. This occurred in Rainford when, following the discovery of a seventeenth-century ceramic drinking cup, the Rainford's Roots project was started. This HLF-funded (Heritage Lottery Fund) community project led by Merseyside Archaeology Society and the Museum of Liverpool revealed an important pottery and clay tobacco pipe industry in Rainford. One vessel, found by chance while digging up a pear tree, lead to the rediscovery of the archaeology of a small but important village.

44. Silver groat of Philip and Mary (LVPL-B46845)
Early Post-Medieval (AD 1554–1558)
Discovered in 2012 in St Helens. Diameter 24 mm.

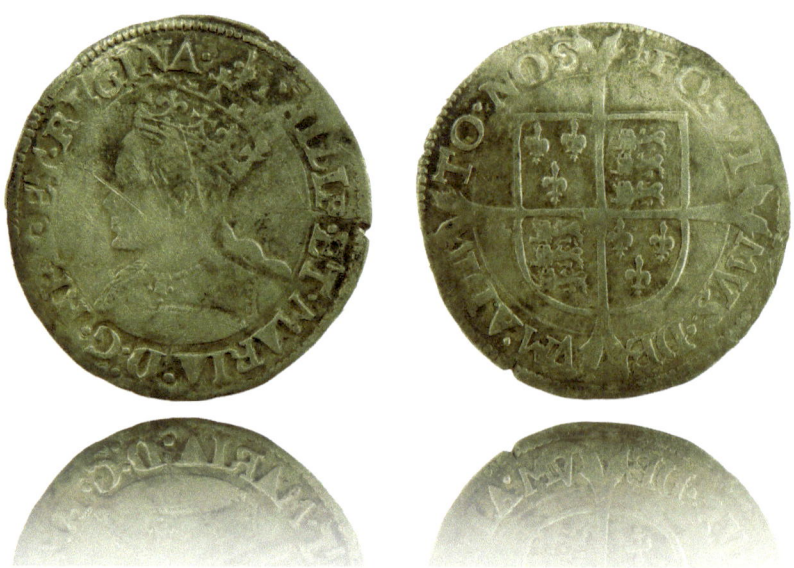

This groat of Philip and Mary was minted at the Tower of London. On the obverse face we can read '*PHILIP ET MARIA D G REX ET REGINA*', which translates as 'Philip and Mary by the Grace of God King and Queen of England'. Depicted is the crowned bust of Mary, facing left. On the reverse of the coin we can read, '*POSVIMVS DEVM ADIVTO NOS*', which translates as 'We have made God our helper'. The legend surrounds a cross fourchée over the royal shield. At the start of the legend on each face is a fleur-de-lis. This is the mint mark for the coin, which narrows down the dates and lets us know where it was made.

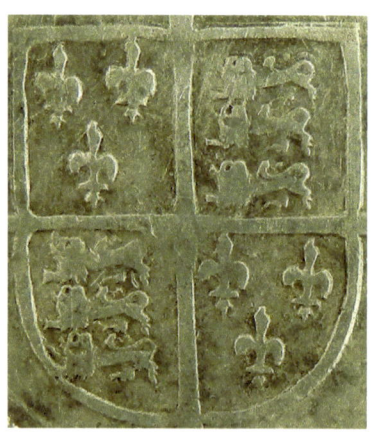

45. Silver-gilt dress fastener (LVPL-4A0113/2014 T71)
Early Post-Medieval (AD 1500–1650)
Discovered in 2012 in Rainford and acquired by the Museum of Liverpool. Diameter 21.96 mm.

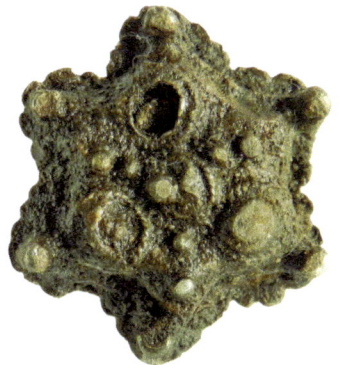 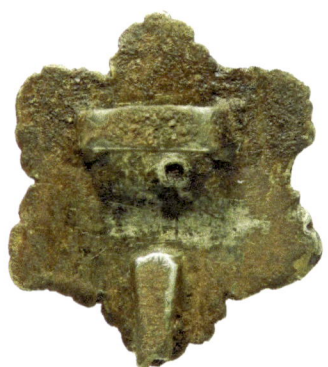

Dress hooks were both practical objects to close clothing and decorative objects to display wealth and fashions. This silver-gilt dress-hook has six lobes with a back plate attached to it, which is a hexagonal cushion with decorative domes and filigree wire. On the reverse is a transverse attachment bar, under which is a hole. This hole may have accommodated a pin that secured an additional decorative element to the front, now missing. Below the hole is the top of the hook, which snapped off following discovery. The decorative gilding and silver surface of the object have been obscured and damaged due to the find being placed in olive oil after discovery. This 'home-made' treatment of finds often results in damaging the object unnecessarily. It is hoped that, following conservation, this find can be returned to its former beauty.

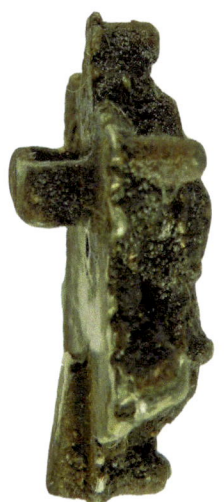

46. Copper-alloy spur (LVPL-18BE69)
Post-Medieval (AD 1600–1700)
Discovered in 2014 in Bebington. Length 81.61 mm.

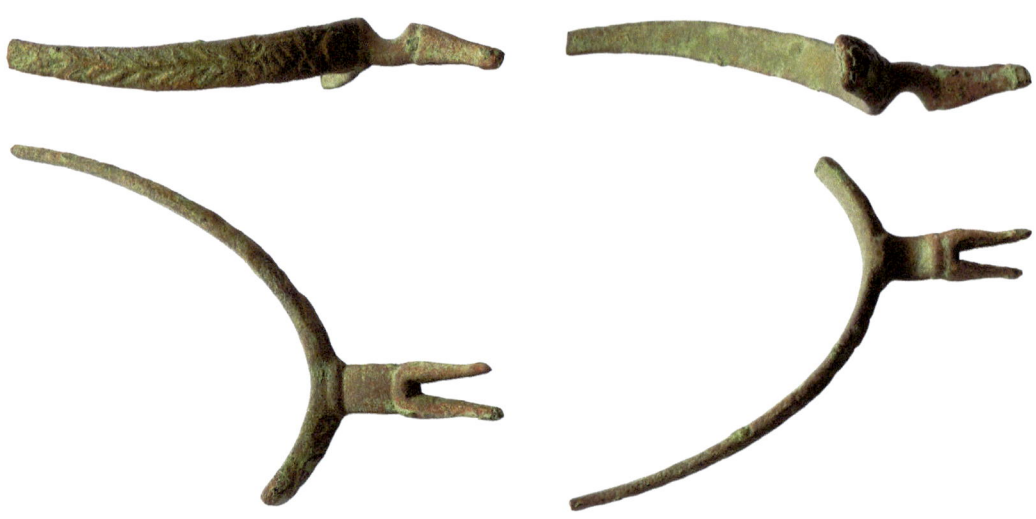

This spur is U-shaped, and the arms are oval in cross-section. Both arms of the spur are broken, and one is considerably shorter than the other. The rowel box is separated from the arms of the spur by a collar and projects from the rear. The arms are decorated with a foliate pattern on their outer face, and the entire object is covered in a mid-green patina. Spurs become decorative in the seventeenth century when they moved from function to fashion, in line with the civil war and post-Restoration dandy style.

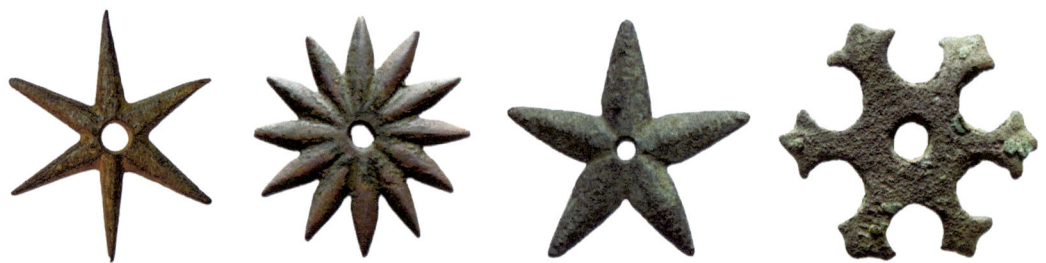

Various types of rowells used with medieval and post-medieval spurs.

47. Glass bead (LVPL-0157C5)
Post-Medieval to Modern (AD 1700–1950)
Discovered in 2014 in Heswall. Length 17 mm.

This bead is made of a monochrome opaque yellow glass with small bubbles. Laid onto the body are two polychrome trails, flush to the surface. Both trails were applied in short zigzags, but not twisted. This very colourful and versatile group is sometimes referred to as 'Fancy or Exotic beads' or sometimes as 'Gololo'. The use of the zigzag cabling on the bead suggests that it was made using lampwork, where a torch or lamp is used to melt the glass. Trade beads such as this, often produced in Venice, were predominantly used in African trade, originally forming the barter in exchange for slaves to be taken to the Caribbean.

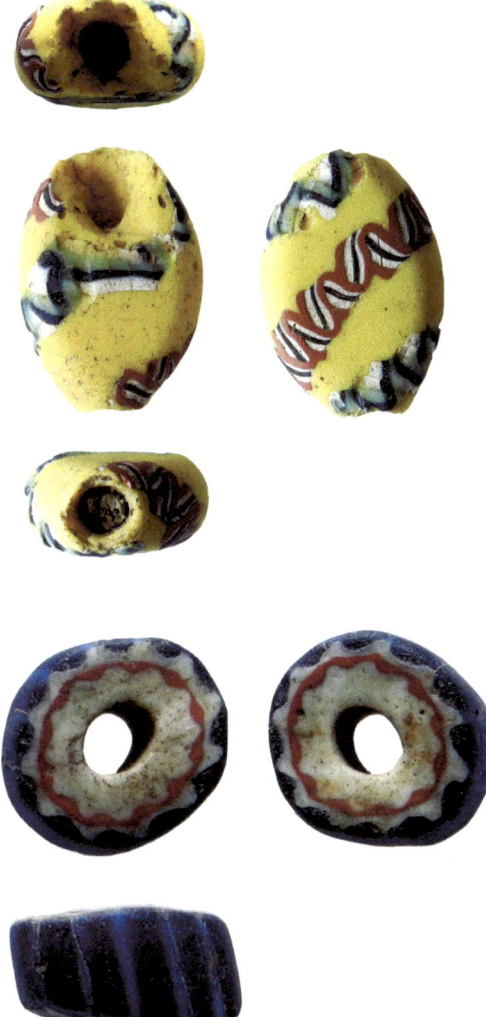

LVPL-0140D2 This bead belongs to a large group of beads known as 'Chevron' beads produced in Venice in a number of Conterie workshops. Chevron beads are found from the fifteenth century onwards. From the 1990s onwards, a number of African and Indian workshops have experimented with copying the beads. Although found all over the world, in Africa they are known as *Bakim-Mutum*. These beads are thought to be imbued with power in some West African tribes and are used as symbols of chieftainship or kingship, or as talismans for witch-healers.

48. Ceramic multi-faceted vessel (LVPL-5D58CD) MOL.2013.127
Post-Medieval (AD 1600–1700)
Discovered in the 1990s in Rainford, acquired by Museum of Liverpool. Height 196 mm.

This multi-faceted drinking cup or 'tyg' has a long conical body, which flares outwards slightly below the handle before tapering the circular base. The cup leans slightly to one side, while one handle and a sherd from the rim are missing. It was discarded following its creation after distorting during firing in the kiln. The cup was discovered in a back garden in Rainford and was subsequently brought into the Museum of Liverpool in 2010.

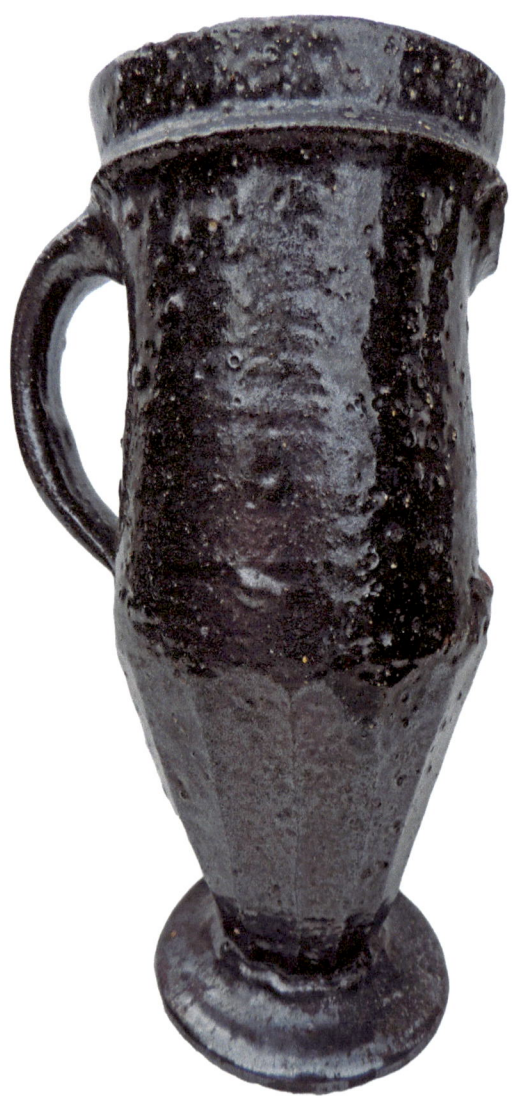

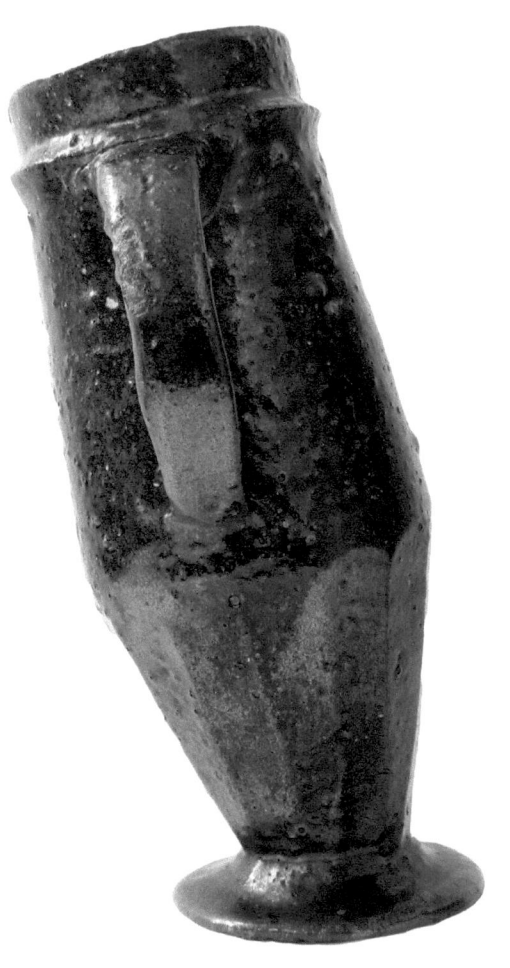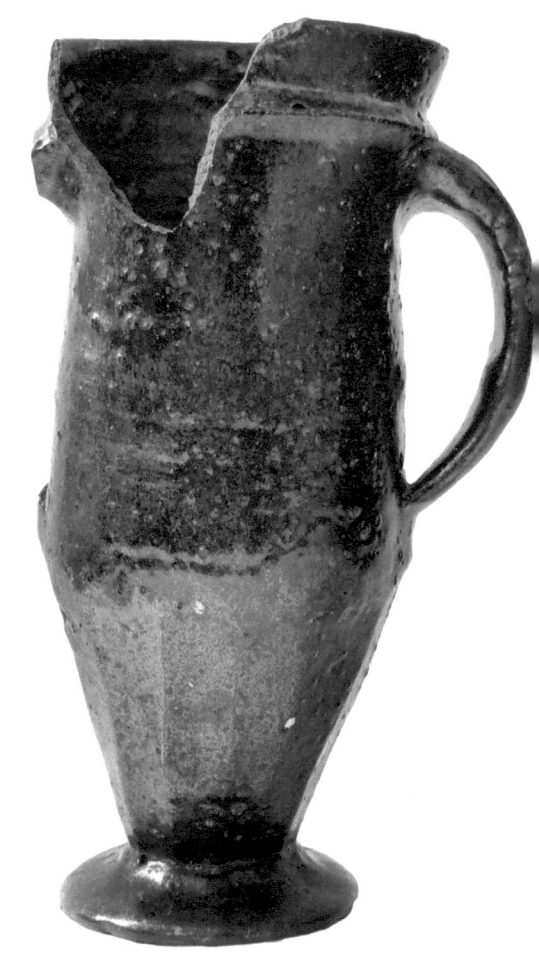

49. Copper-alloy toy cannon (LVPL-AB8742)
Post-Medieval (AD 1690–1750)
Discovered in 2008 in Sefton. Length 95.32 mm.

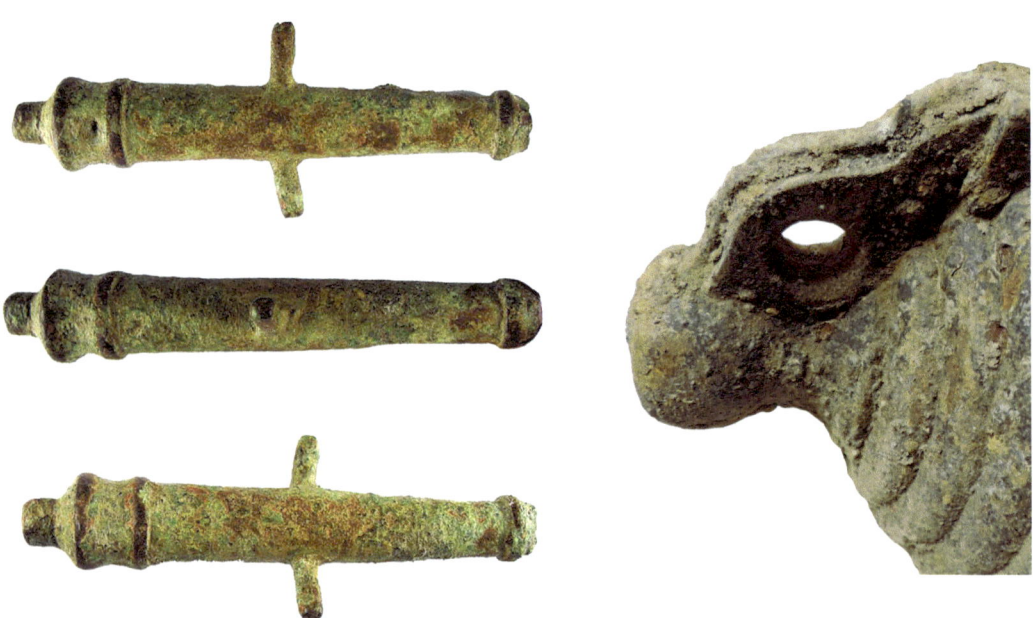

Miniature toy cannons were popular in the post-medieval period. This cannon has two trunnions protruding from either side of the barrel, which would have allowed the object to be mounted on a carriage. The vent hole is corroded over and there is a reinforcement band on either side. The carriage is no longer present; it would have likely been made of wood, meaning it would not easily be preserved. These toys were produced as working models of their larger counterparts, such as the example seen below, discovered on a building site in Liverpool.

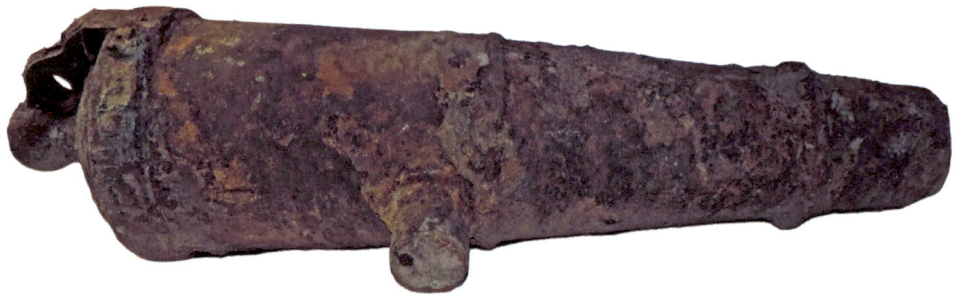

MOL.2007.50.200: Full-sized cannon discovered on a building site in Liverpool.

50. Clay pipe (LVPL-DA3308)
Modern (AD 1880–1990)
Discovered in 2011 in Upton. Length 54.65 mm.

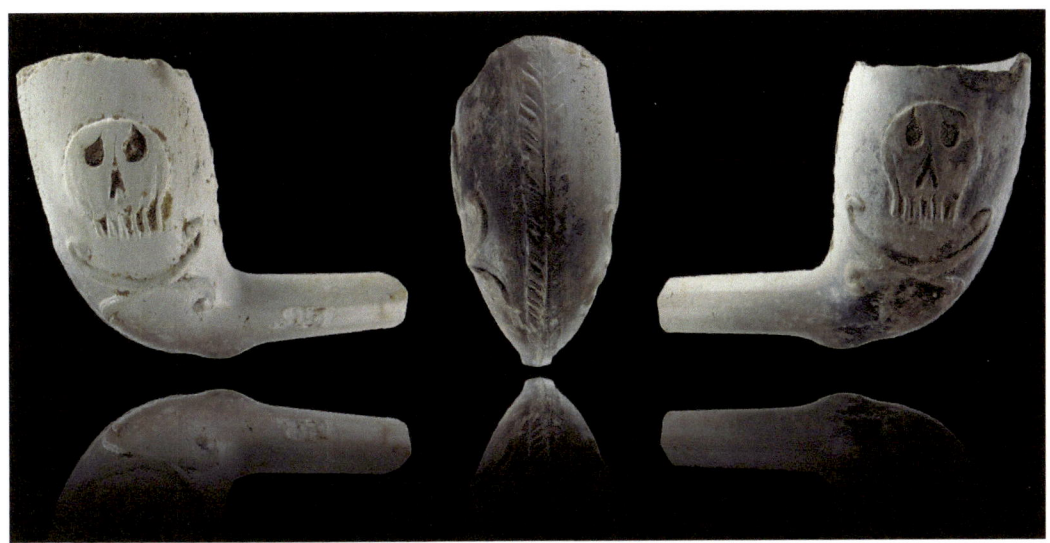

This moulded clay tobacco pipe bowl and stem has been decorated with a 'skull and crossbones' symbol on both sides. More decorative moulding is present along the mould seam line, with a diagonal leaf pattern. The rim of the bowl has been damaged and a broken spur remains on the base of the bowl. A possible maker's mark is present on the left-hand side of the stem, close to the bowl, consisting of two letters or numbers, possibly '95'. Clay-pipe specialist David Higgins has identified this as a product from the Pollock factory in Manchester. This business was founded by Edward Pollock in 1879 and operated under three successive generations until its sale in 1990.

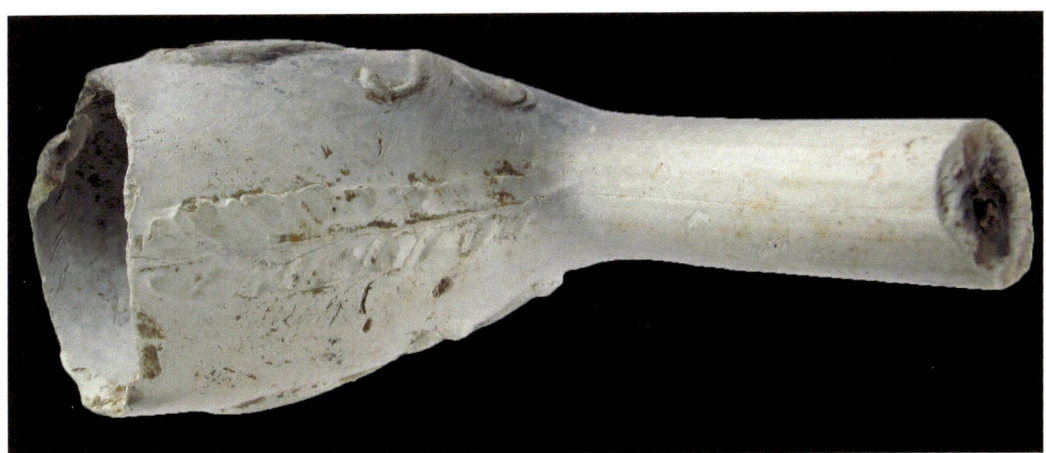

Concluding Thoughts

Just some of the objects recorded with the Portable Antiquities Scheme in Manchester and Merseyside have been highlighted in this volume. By exploring the PAS database (www.finds.org.uk/database), you can find many more interesting objects discovered throughout England and Wales. The current city and suburban landscape allows for few new chance finds. This makes it all the more important that when objects are discovered they are recorded, in order that we, and future generations, can all benefit and learn from them. Advances in technology are constantly changing how we connect with the past. Advances in cameras, recording equipment and drone technology make it quicker and easier to record archaeological sites. Likewise, changing technology is affecting the recovery of chance finds. After discovering a significant object, I'm often told the field has been 'gone over' hundreds of times before, but that this time a new detector had been used or the site had been deep ploughed by the farmer. Deep ploughing often leads to the destruction of archaeology before it can be recorded. Through the recording of metal-detected finds and the careful plotting of their find spots, some of this unique archaeological data can

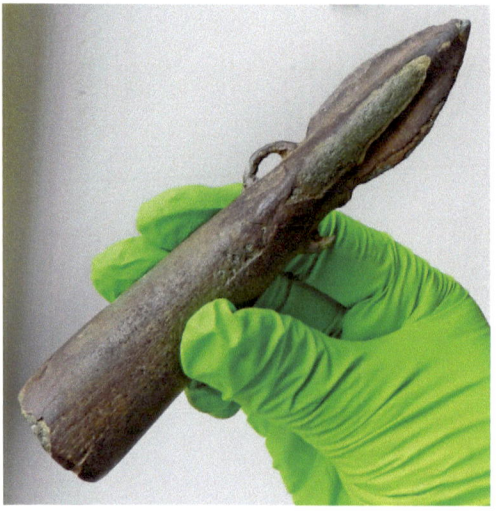

be saved. How that data is recorded is also changing. Grid references, once difficult to pin down accurately on a paper map, especially when attempting to do so in a windy field, have largely been replaced by handheld GPS. These are in turn are being replaced by often free GPS apps for smartphones, providing researchers with more reliable information. Technology can also change how we interact with those objects once they are recovered, enabling us to view them in 3D or through virtual-reality headsets.

It is often stated that archaeology is destruction and, once removed from the ground, it is essential that excavation reports are published so that the information recovered is not lost. Likewise it is necessarily to record chance finds. Like a giant jigsaw puzzle, when we piece together the dots that are single objects on a map, they tell a story; patterns emerge indicating where people lived, worked and traded. The objects themselves reveal to us the technology of the past, and trends in fashion and wealth. By recording objects, finders are ensuring that all of this information can be captured for future generations to enjoy, explore and connect with. Recording where the object was discovered is central to this. As new stories emerge from the soil every week, we will continue to work together to make sure they can be told.

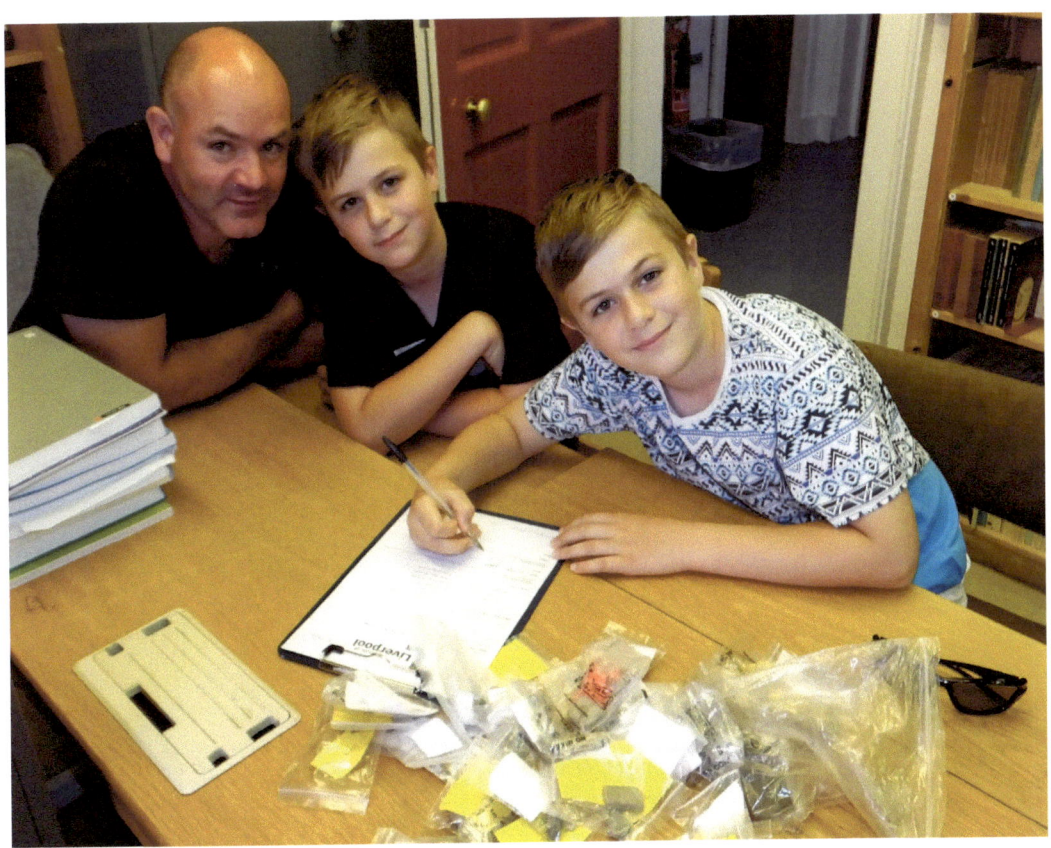

Young metal detectorists George (left) and Harry (right) Fowles with their dad Bryan, recording their finds with PAS.

Further Reading

Bailey, R., Oakden, V. and Okasha, E., 'A pre-conquest Latin inscription from North-West England' *Medieval Archaeology Vol. 56* (Maney Publishing, 2012).

Boughton, D., *50 Finds from Cumbria: Objects from the Portable Antiquities Scheme* (Gloucestershire: Amberley, 2016).

Cherry, J., 'A Medieval Gold brooch found in Manchester' in *Volume I Medieval Manchester* (Manchester: Manchester Archaeological Unit, 1983).

Griffiths, D., *Vikings of the Irish Sea* (Gloucestershire: The History Press, 2010).

Griffiths, D., Philpott, R. and Egan, G., *Meols: The Archaeology of the North Wirral Coast* (Oxford: Oxford University School of Archaeology, 2007).

Margeson, S.M., *Norwich Households: Medieval and Post-Medieval Finds from Norwich Survey Excavations 1971–78* (Norwich: East Anglian Archaeology, 1993).

Picard, J. and R., *Chevron and Nueva Cadiz beads. Beads from the West African Trade Volume VII* (California: Carmel, 1993).

Lewis, A., *Iron Age and Roman-Era Vehicle Terrets from Western and Central Britain: an Interpretive Study* (Leicester: School of Archaeology and Ancient History University of Leicester, 2015).

Miller, I. and Aldridge, B., *Greater Manchester Revealed* (Oxford Archaeology Ltd, 2011).

Miller, I. and Wild, C., *Hell upon Earth the Archaeology of Angel Meadow* (Oxford: Oxford Archaeology Ltd, 2015).

Nevell, M., 'The Boothsbank Roman Coin Hoard' in the *Seaby Coin and Medal Bulletin 851* (for June 1990).

Nevell, M., *Manchester: The Hidden History* (Gloucestershire: The History Press, 2008).

Oakden, V., *50 Finds from Cheshire: Objects from the Portable Antiquities Scheme* (Gloucestershire: Amberley, 2015).

Oswald, A., 'Clay Pipes for the Archaeologist', *British Archaeological Report 14* (Oxford: 1975).

Shotter, D., *Roman Coins from North-West England: First Supplement* (Lancaster: Lancaster University, 1995).

Shotter, D., *Roman Coins from North-West England: Third Supplement* (Lancaster: Lancaster University, 2011).

Stewart, L. and Oakden, V., *Romano-British Treasures of Cheshire* (National Museums Liverpool, 2016).